HELIOS

Volume 48   Fall 2021   Number 2

Entanglements of the Human and Nonhuman in Euripides' *Helen*   79
  Maria Combatti

Language and Agency in Sappho's Brothers Poem   113
  Alexandra Leewon Schultz

Reframing Iphis and Caeneus: Trans Narratives and Socio-Linguistic
Gendering in Ovid's *Metamorphoses*   145
  J. L. Watson

Notes on Contributors   175

HELIOS

EDITOR
Steven M. Oberhelman

EDITORIAL BOARD

Helene Foley Barnard	Mary-Kay Gamel California, Santa Cruz	Barbara K. Gold Hamilton
S. C. Humphreys Michigan	W. R. Johnson Chicago	Richard P. Martin Stanford
Sheila Murnaghan Pennsylvania	Martha Nussbaum Chicago	C. Robert Phillips III Lehigh
Brent Shaw Princeton	Marilyn Skinner Arizona	Victoria Wohl Toronto

HELIOS publishes articles that explore innovative approaches to the study of classical culture, literature, and society. Especially welcome are articles that embrace contemporary critical methodologies, such as anthropological, deconstructive, feminist, reader response, social history, and text theory.

Authors are encouraged to send an electronic copy of their paper (preferably as a PDF file) to the editor. An abstract of at least 150 words should accompany the article. **All manuscripts must be anonymous, with no reference to the author appearing in the text or notes, and will be refereed by experts in the field.**

For standard titles and abbreviations of ancient sources, the author should consult LSJ^9, OLD, and OCD^3. For bibliographical citations, the author must follow the author-date format; the format may be found in the style-sheet in *TAPA*.

Please address all editorial correspondence to Steven M. Oberhelman, Editor, Dept. of International Studies, Texas A&M University, College Station, Texas 77843-4215; email: s-oberhelman@tamu.edu.

Subscriptions are $64.00 for individuals ($89.00 outside the U.S.) and $108.00 for institutions ($164.00 outside the U.S.). Payment in U.S. currency, check, money order, or bank draft drawn on a U.S. bank should be made payable to Texas Tech University Press.

Helios–ISSN 0160-0923
Fall 2021, Volume 48, no. 2
(published two times a year)
Copyright © 2021
Texas Tech University Press
Box 41037
Lubbock, Texas 79409-1037

Subscriptions and other business matters should be addressed to
Texas Tech University Press
Attn: Journal Subscriptions
Phone: 806.742.2982
Box 41037
Lubbock, TX 79409-1037 USA
Email: ttup@ttu.edu

Entanglements of the Human and Nonhuman in Euripides' *Helen*

MARIA COMBATTI

Abstract

This article explores depictions and perceptions of Helen's relations with the nonhuman world. Drawing on the insights of posthumanism, new materialisms, and affect theory for interpretative assistance, it argues that Helen, animals, natural entities, and material things are interconnected in bundles of intra-actions and trans-corporeal entanglements, which make Helen's embodied, emotional experience vividly perceptible to the audience. Three things are exemplary in this regard: the "lovely virgin streams" (καλλιπάρθενοι ῥοαί, 1) of the Nile, whose features merge with Helen's physical and moral qualities; the "egg" (τεῦχος νεοσσῶν λευκὸν, 256), which materializes her feeling of being a "monstrosity" (τέρας, 255); and the "statue" (ἄγαλμα, 262), which Helen compares to herself to bewail her beauty. Thus, by reacting to the Leitmotiv of the *eidōlon* ("phantom") and highlighting the protean atmosphere of the Egyptian setting, this article aims to show that reading the *Helen* with a focus on the entanglements of the human and nonhuman allows us to shed new light on the theme of doubling, indeterminacy, and multiplicity which underlies the play.

Helen is traditionally associated with animals, especially birds, natural entities, and material things. She has an avian lineage, being born from Zeus's rape of her mother in the form of a swan and having hatched out from an egg. In the palinodic version of her myth, which Euripides follows in his play, her appearance is confused with that of her *eidōlon* ("phantom"), which went to Troy in her place.[1] Material things, such as robes, statues, and ships, also play an important role in Helen's story. In *Iliad* 3 Helen weaves "a great twofold purple web" (ἡ δὲ μέγαν ἱστὸν ὕφαινε / δίπλακα πορφυρέην, 125–126) on which she embroiders the battles between Achaeans and Trojans, and in *Odyssey* 15 she gives the most beautiful of

---

1. Helen's *eidōlon* seems to have been present in the so-called Palinode of Stesichorus, in which the poet claims that not Helen, but her phantom went to Troy. Herodotus also endorses the version of Helen's myth in which she went to Egypt rather than Troy (2.112–120). For a discussion on these versions, see Allan 2008, 18–28.

her "richly embroidered robes" (οἱ πέπλοι παμποίκιλοι, 105) to Telemachus as "a remembrance of her hands" (μνῆμ' Ἑλένης χειρῶν, 105–126) for his future bride. In his *Agamemnon*, Aeschylus reveals that there were "beautiful statues" (εὐμόρφων δὲ κολοσσῶν, 416) of Helen in her palace, which were hateful to Menelaus during her wife's absence. Finally, Helen's name encapsulates a striking pun for which she was called "destroyer of ships, men, and cities" (ἑλένας, ἕλανδρος, ἑλέπτολις, *Ag.* 688–689), in relation to the tragic events of the Trojan War. In the *Helen*, Euripides uses all these entities (egg, *eidōlon*, robes, statues, ships) afresh to both react against the traditional version of the myth and challenge the audience's expectations about Helen's behavior and attitude.

    The play tells the story of Helen, who was snatched by Hermes and then transported to Egypt, while her *eidōlon*, a phantom fashioned by Hera from the air, followed Paris to Troy. In Egypt, Helen confines herself to the tomb of the King Proteus as a suppliant in order to protect herself from the clutches of the new King Theoclymenus, who wants to marry her. Talking and singing to the chorus made of Greek women who had been abducted by pirates and brought to Egypt, she laments her situation by telling the story of her rape and blaming her beauty for causing the Trojan War. Then, when Menelaus arrives in Egypt and they are reunited, Helen helps him and the shipwrecked Greeks to return home, by convincing Theoclymenus to give them a ship, on which she herself embarks. Once in Greece, she ends her life on an island close to Attica which will take her name. As Helene Foley (2001, 205) has observed, Euripides in this play presents a virtuous Helen, who has been abducted and finally returns to a renewed reputation, bringing with her a mitigation of the past suffering and destruction.[2] In this article, I explore how the nonhuman world, including animals, natural entities, and material things, is implicated in Helen's dramatic experience of abduction and redemption, and show how this relationship draws the spectators into the circuit of her feelings and emotions.[3]

---

    2. By drawing a parallelism with the myth of Persephone, Foley argues that the *Helen* is an "*anodos* drama" about a woman who experiences a loss of previous identity followed by a return to a renewed marriage and reputation. For a bibliography and an overview of the play's interpretations, see Segal 1971, Bassi 1987, Austin 1994, Burian 2007, Allan 2008, Burian and Shapiro 2011, Blondell 2013, Marshall 2014, Boedecker 2017.

    3. I draw on the insights of posthumanism and new materialisms to investigate the relationship between Helen and the nonhuman world. This investigation emphasizes a de-centration of the human and foregrounds nonhuman agency, reacting against a subjectivist approach that sees a hierarchical distinction between person and thing. I also engage with affect theory, which not only highlights nonhuman agency but also redefines emotion as a material force that passes from bodies to bodies, both animate and inanimate. For a detailed discussion on my engagement with the posthumanism, new materialisms, and affect theory, see below.

Introduction: Helen and the Nonhuman World

The *Helen* has been studied extensively, but I argue that a focus on Helen's relations with the nonhuman world reveals important aspects of the play that have not been appreciated. Entanglements with nonhuman entities involve many characters in Greek tragedy.[4] However, a different and peculiar situation emerges for Helen, not only because she herself is more than human, moving fluidly between the divine, human, and animal categories, but also because in our play she is confused with a phantom and acts in the exotic and protean environment of Egypt, which allows for a strong blurring of humans (Helen as well as the chorus women) and nonhumans.[5] The story of the *eidōlon* has led scholars to underline Helen's association with the nonhuman world, generating prolific discussions about the relationship between appearance and reality in the play.[6] Naomi Weiss (2018, 140–190) has investigated how Helen and the chorus merge with a succession of singing and dancing birds: the Sirens in the *parodos*, the nightingale in the first *stasimon*, and the cranes in the third *stasimon*. Other scholars have discussed the remarkable use of theatrical stuff in the play, concentrating attention on props, costumes, and stage items. Sarah Powers, for instance, has argued (2010) that just as Helen uses theatrical properties to revise her story, Euripides deploys theatrical materials in order to push the play towards the comic genre.[7] Erika Weiberg in her own turn has investigated (2020) how Proteus's tomb replaces the *eidōlon* as a material sign, functioning as a potent stage property that becomes central to Helen's and Menelaus's recognition and their escape from Egypt. Whereas these studies provide productive readings of the philosophical perspectives, performative and musical characteristics, and functionality and materiality of theatrical stuff in the play, in this article I propose to trace the unique and nuanced ways in which Helen and the chorus women are immersed in the play's physical environment, such that their bodies and selves become an integral part of that environment. In doing so, I show that the merging of the environment with the women impinges not only on the

---

4. See Rehm 2002 on the relationship between tragic bodies and the theatrical and natural space. See also the essays in Telò and Mueller 2018 as well as Worman 2020 in regard to the interrelation between tragic characters, affects, and materialities.

5. For a discussion on the Egyptian setting in the play, see Segal 1971; Wright 2005, 163–202; Weiss 2018, 140–190. In my discussion about Helen's entanglements with the nonhuman world I also include the chorus women, who share the same experience of abduction with Helen, as said above.

6. See Segal 1971, Pucci 1997, Gumpert 2001, Allan 2008, Zeitlin 2010, Boedecker 2017.

7. The general scholarly consensus about *Helen*'s genre seems to be that of a mixture and interplay of tragedy and comedy which allowed Euripides to experiment in some way, by incorporating the elements of a completely different genre. For a discussion, see Dunn 1996; Wright 2005, 228–235; Allan 2008, 66–72; Jansen 2012, 328; Marshall 2014, 55; Zuckerberg 2016.

plot, action, and genre, but also on the affective engagement of the spectators. Thus, I demonstrate that the wondrous Egyptian setting—where the waters of the Nile reflect human feelings and emotions; the surrounding flora coalesces with human bodies; Helen meshes with things such as the egg, statue, and ship; and nonhuman actors (e.g., statue and mask) intersect with each other—represents a surreal but materially palpable landscape of intertwined interrelationships between humans and nonhumans which renders Helen's and the chorus women's dramatic experience deeply involving the audience.

My analysis of the play combines a philological method (close readings of the text) with contemporary critical approaches (posthumanism, new materialisms, and affect theory) in order to interpret dramatic perspectives. Before embarking on the examination of specific passages, it is worth outlining in more detail the theoretical framework within which I place my argumentation. First, I engage with the insights of the posthumanism which question the boundaries between the human and nonhuman and observe that humans and other beings (both animate and inanimate) intersect and coalesce.[8] Who more than Helen, whose identity meshes with that of the *eidōlon*, does best exemplify this conception? Bearing this question in mind, I explore here "intra-actions" and "trans-corporeal" entanglements of human and nonhuman entities, examining how Helen, the chorus women, animals, natural entities, and material things are interconnected in a mutual constitution of agencies and bodily enmeshments.[9] For instance, I examine how Helen and the Sirens

---

8. For an overview of posthuman theories, see Grusin 2015 (on the so-called nonhuman turn) and Seaman 2007 (on more-than-human theories). See also the essays collected in the volume edited by Vint (2020), which provides an overview of how theory and criticism under the framework of posthumanism have transformed humanities scholarship today. For an overview of posthuman studies of the antiquity and classical literature, see Bianchi et al. 2019 and Chesi and Spiegel 2020. The problematical consideration of any kind of entities and matter as nonhuman has also been noted (Harman 2018, 244) and criticized (Rekret 2016, Sofer 2016). Space does not allow me to fully engage with this debate, but I think that it is necessary to calibrate the rhetoric of the posthumanism in "a more historically nuanced way," as Goldhill (2020, 341) says. In this light, I place posthuman theories in dialogue with the ancient conceptions of the interrelations between humans and the wider environment (e.g., the notion of *zōē*, that is, the kind of life that for the Greeks encompassed animals, plants, the cosmos, and the divine in addition to the human), and highlight the importance that the nonhuman world had in Greek culture. Also, my reading of the *Helen* includes resourcing posthumanism with a historical depth, by exploring human and nonhuman entanglements vis-à-vis the cultural, social, and material context of Athens, in which the play was set.

9. The term *intra-action* is from Barad 2007, 140, who refers to the material world as a realm of interconnected agencies and continuous interplay between humans and nonhuman entities. The term *trans-corporeality* is borrowed from Alaimo 2010, 63, who defines it as "a conception of the body that is neither essentialist, nor genetically determined, nor firmly bounded, but rather a body in which social power and material/geographic agencies intra-act." Alaimo uses the concept

(birdlike creature companions of Persephone who join Helen in her lament for rape) share the same embodied hybrid nature, finding themselves part of a world of grief and abuse. Furthermore, I consider the ways in which the natural entities (lands, rivers, and plants) existing in the Egyptian landscape merge with Helen's and the chorus women's bodies and selves. Finally, I focus on objects and material things like Helen's egg, which actively engage with the heroine's action and are inextricably entangled with her being and identity.

By highlighting the exotic setting of Egypt, Matthew Wright (2005, 158–224) has observed that the *Helen* is one of Euripides' "escape-tragedies" that relies on "an idealized imaginary landscape which reflects the characters' own identity and situations." I go a step further in pointing out the relationship between the Egyptian landscape and the characters, exploring how Helen's and the chorus women's corporeality and emotions converge with the natural world.[10] The Nile's waters and reeds, whose features intertwine with the bodies and feelings of Helen and the chorus, are remarkable examples of the blurring of the natural world with the women characters. In the context of these human-nature interactions, the Egyptian landscape is not completely estranged from the Greek landscape; indeed, the characteristics of the Nile, its waters, and surrounding vegetation recall those of the Eurotas River in Sparta, on whose banks, as the myth says, Helen used to lead marriage rites. Moreover, the play concludes with the deification of Helen, which elides into the blending of her identity into a Greek island. In these terms, Euripides depicts a material, protean landscape where natural forces overlap with personal, emotional, and socio-cultural dynamics.[11]

---

of trans-corporeality to express the sense of the human as embedded in material environments and flows of the world; see Alaimo 2020, 177–191. Drawing on this conception, I use trans-corporeality for human (women)-nonhuman interactions which take into account interconnected forms of embodiment. The more generic term *entanglement* is from Hodder 2012, who uses it in the archeological setting to demonstrate how humans and things are enabled and constrained in bundles of heterogonous interdependences.

10. My reading of the relationship between the women characters and the natural world is grounded in the ancient theory of the human body as a microcosm being conceived from the same elements as the rest of the universe. Greek thinkers from Pythagoras to Aristotle viewed the cosmos as a living organism made of the same stuff as human bodies. This theory explains why in Greek literature natural entities, such as wind, water, and plants are often used to describe the human self and conversely why human concepts are applied to natural entities. For an overview of Greek thinkers' conceptions of space and the cosmos, see Rehm 2002, 273–296. In the late fifth century, Presocratic philosophy and Hippocratic medicine also offered model conceptions for explaining questions of human nature. As Holmes (2017, 34) observes, "In the classical period the physical body works as the bridge between inquiries into nonhuman things and stuffs and new inquiries into nature of people as both biological beings and social agents."

11. Haraway (2003) uses the term *natureculture*, which illustrates how the natural is entwined in a complex dynamic with the social and cultural. Schliephake (2020) has argued that ancient

In my investigation of Helen's entanglements with nonhuman entities, I also include objects or material things, such as robes, statues, and ships, which operate as vital agents in the play. In exploring their function, I draw on the insights of the so-called new materialisms, which have placed emphasis on the ontological status of objects with interest in their agency, allure, and vitality.[12] Scholars of classics have discussed the function of material objects in Greek literature and art in accordance with ancient aesthetic and cultural parameters.[13] In regard to ancient drama, Melissa Mueller (2016) has interpreted theatrical objects (props, costumes, and set pieces) as "actors," highlighting their essential role in the staging and reception of Greek tragedy. Following up these studies, I take into consideration both onstage and offstage objects, by focusing attention on their participation in the play's action. For instance, I show how the "shrouds" (ὑφάσματα, 1243) that Helen uses for Menelaus's fake burial act as material agents that help her deceive Theoclymenus and consequently renew her reputation in the eyes of Menelaus and the Greek people.[14] Moreover, I look closely at the ways in which Helen's body morphs into objects, giving life to "assemblages," which, in the words of Jane Bennett (2010, 24), "include humans, their social constructions, and some powerful nonhumans." An excellent example in this respect is the *agalma* ("statue," 262), which becomes the material equivalent of Helen's body, intersecting with her personal and social experience of woman and wife.

As new materialists have observed, objects are also vibrant entities that materialize the emotional transactions between human subjects.[15] Mario Telò and Melissa Mueller (2018) have underscored how this view has fostered a new, theoretically grounded interest in the affective exchange between performers (humans and objects) and audience in ancient theatrical settings. Building on such insights and

---

religion made up the encounter between nature and culture. I consider human (in this case women's) bodies and emotions as an integral part of this encounter. In this context, I especially examine how the motif of rape generates a sense of trans-corporeality, a recognition that the women's bodies and feelings are vitally connected to the broader environment, where social, cultural, and natural forces intersect. See also Vasunia 2001, 72, who observes how, by and large, Euripides exoticizes and reshapes Egypt, especially in relation to racial and gender aspects.

12. See Bennett 2010, Brown 2004 and 2015, Harman 2002 and 2018.

13. For an overview and bibliography on the new materialisms and classics, see Canevaro 2019.

14. Latour (2004) and Mol (2010) use the notion of Actor Network Theory (ANT) to explain how humans and things exist in constantly shifting networks of relationships in the social and natural worlds. In these terms, I regard Helen and material actors as parts of an all-encompassing natural-material-cultural network in which they are entangled in a mutual constitution of agencies.

15. See Brown 2004 and 2015. On the "affective turn" in critical theory, see Clough and Halley 2007, and Gregg and Seigworth 2010.

extending my investigation to the many nonhuman entities inhabiting the theatrical space and the imaginary landscape, I show how in the *Helen* the blurring of the human and nonhuman actors increases the diffusion of feelings and emotions, and elicit powerful affective responses in the audience.[16] Therefore, I examine how intra-actions and trans-corporeal entanglements of Helen, the chorus women, animals, plants, rivers, and objects activate sensorial phenomena (visual, aural, and tactile) which enhance the spectators' embodied, cognitive, and emotional involvement in the dramatic events and women characters' experiences.[17]

In what follows, I individuate five patterns of human and nonhuman entanglements that demonstrate how the interconnectedness of Helen, the chorus women, and other beings is vital to the play. I show not only how Helen and the chorus women describe animals, natural entities, and material things to express their own feelings and emotions, but also how they all actively intersect and coalesce. All five sections taken together permit us to read the *Helen* through a conceptualization of the dramatic performance formed out of an ongoing flow of intra-actions and trans-corporeal entanglements of the human and nonhuman worlds. This reading ultimately provides a new understanding of the theme of doubling, indeterminacy,

---

16. I point to an experienced audience that would appreciate both the theatrical performance and the verbal communication, thereby considering the appeal of both onstage materials (props, masks, costumes, set pieces) and the subtleties of the script, like metaphors, intra-textual references, and intertextual allusions. I am aware that things seen on stage have a greater claim to perception. Yet, it is worth foregrounding the exceptional nature of the dramatic performance, which encompasses theatrical materials, embodied enactment, music, and language altogether. Thus, I examine how the play's onstage material environment and visualizing language interrelate with each other to give the spectators a full picture of Helen's and the chorus women's dramatic experience. For a discussion on the ancient audience's competence, through an approach that considers both the linguistic level of the spoken words and paralinguistic and visual signs (gestures, costumes, music), see Revermann 2006. On tragic language, embodied enactment, and visual dimension of the ancient dramatic performance, see Segal 1980 and 1993; Zeitlin 1994; Goldhill 2000, 164–165; Taplin 2003, 1–6; Kraus et al. 2007.

17. I place recent works in classical scholarship, marked by the publication of the series *The Senses in Antiquity* (Bradley and Butler 2014–2019), in dialogue with the insights of the new materialisms, which have complemented the study of ancient material things and artifacts by emphasizing sensuous and aesthetic forces (Porter 2010 and 2016, Gaifman and Platt 2018). These conceptions tie in well with recent theories inspired by the so-called enactive approach to cognition, which makes a compelling case for visualization (i.e., the spectators' imagination of things spoken or sung) as relating to the active embodied structure of experience. See Thompson 2007 and Grethlein and Huitink 2017. On cognitive approaches to classical drama, see Meineck et al. 2019 and Anderson et al. 2018. On the drama's various strategies to solicit the audience's engagement and on the forms of interest employed by the spectators themselves, see Roselli 2011. For an overview of the poetics of emotional expression, philosophical theories of emotion, and the role of material culture in the representation of ancient affectivity, see Cairns and Nelis 2017. For an overview on emotions in Greek tragedy, see Konstan 2006, Chaniotis 2012, Stanford 2014.

and multiplicity which underlies the play, throwing light on the peculiar features of Euripides' artistry.

I The Nile's Waters and Reeds

The play begins with a prologue in which Helen tells the audience that her body was seized by Hermes and brought to Egypt, while her *eidōlon* went to Troy with Paris (1-67). In the first three lines of the prologue, the description of the Nile sets the scene of action, mentally transporting the spectators sitting in the Theater of Dionysus to the land of Egypt:

Νείλου μὲν αἵδε καλλιπάρθενοι ῥοαί   1
ὃς ἀντὶ δίας ψακάδος Αἰγύπτου πέδον
λευκῆς τακείσης χιόνος ὑγραίνει γύας.

These are the lovely virgin streams of the Nile,
which fed by melting white snow drenches the plain of Egypt,
namely its fields in place of rain.[18]

Helen's vivid depiction of the Nile heightens the audience's perceptual awareness of the river and its surrounding environment.[19] First, the deictic αἵδε ("these here") brings the river's streams before the spectators' mind's eye. Next, the references to melting snow activate an embodied, as well as emotional, appeal; in fact, in Greek literature τήκω ("to melt") is often used for bodily manifestations that relate to emotional states. For instance, at *Odyssey* 19.205-209, Penelope's "lovely cheeks" (καλὰ παρήια), which "melt with tears" (τήκετο δάκρυ) as she listens to Odysseus's stories, are compared to the melting snow (χιὼν κατατήκετο) which fills the streams of the rivers (τηκομένης δ'ἄρα τῆς ποταμοὶ πλήθουσι ῥέοντες).[20]

---

18. For the text I use the edition of Allan 2008, with some adaptations. Translations are adapted from Kovacs 2002 and Burian and Shapiro 2011.

19. Wright (2005, 167-202) has pointed out that the Greek characters' "ignorance" of Egyptian geography is amply stressed in the play. However, even if it is not clear how familiar Greek travelers would have been with Egyptian geography, considerable commercial relationships existed between the Greek poleis and the trading cities of the Nile delta, which also led to trace a mythical, ethnic connection through the figure of Io. Thus, the spectators should have had an idea of the Nile's waters.

20. It is worth noting that the Homeric epithet καλλιπάρῃος ("of lovely cheeks"), which derives from the expression καλὰ παρήια and is close to the Euripidean καλλιπάρθενοι, is applied to Helen at *Od.* 15.123, when she gives her gift of a robe to Telemachus. Thus, the depiction of the Nile may hint at an allusion to Homer, highlighting the relationship (also underlined by weaving) between Penelope and Helen as lovely, faithful wives.

Finally, ὑγραίνω ("to drench") is also remarkable. Whereas here the verb refers to the Nile's streams, later in the play Helen uses it for the tears that drenched her eyes (βλέφαρον ὑγραίνω / δάκρυσιν, 673–674) when Hermes abducted her and brought her to the Nile. From these references it seems clear that Helen describes the Nile's waters not only to create a vivid image of the Egyptian environment but also to draw the spectators into the circuit of her feelings.[21]

The depiction of the Nile also provides Helen with the opportunity to revise her implication in the Trojan War. The "lovely virgin streams" (καλλιπάρθενοι ῥοαί) of the Nile are opposite to the Scamander's waters, which, as Helen herself says in the prologue, are "full of dead people" (ψυχαὶ δὲ πολλαὶ [...] ἐπὶ Σκαμανδρίοις / ῥοαῖσιν ἔθανον, 52–53), offering an alternative to the bloody world of Troy.[22] In this manner, we may say that the depiction of the Nile mediates and signifies Helen's innocence, while underlining her suffering and vulnerability. The adjective καλλιπάρθενοι is interesting in this respect. Ruby Blondell (2013, 204) has observed that this rare compound establishes Egypt as the natural home for "beauty" (κάλλος) and virginal purity (πάρθενοι), coexisting in apparent harmony. However, after Proteus's death, Helen lives in Egypt under the threat of Theoclymenus's rape (61–63). Therefore, the adjective not only points up the harmonic relationship between Helen and Egypt in terms of beauty and virtue, but also foregrounds the woman's sexual vulnerability. Indeed, in the play Helen's experience intersects with that of the chorus women and in general reflects the story of the mythical "maidens" (πάρθενοι), who were abducted from the chorus, and of the nymphs fleeing sexual violence.[23] In this way, Helen's embodied self is interconnected with the natural environment, such that her suffering blends into the Nile's waters. This blurring renders Helen's feelings neatly discernible to the

---

21. On the relationship between the Nile's streams and Helen, see Downing 1990 and Zweig 1999.

22. On the opposition between the Nile and Scamander's waters in the *Helen*, see Vasunia 2001, 61.

23. On the prologue's as well as the *parodos*'s motif of abduction and rape which likens Helen to mythic maidens, see Juffras 1993. This association also recalls Helen's traditional connection to parthenaic performances and marriages rites. Parthenaic performances relate to rape, as gatherings and circling dances of maidens were often depicted as groups of *parthenoi* from which a chosen woman was snatched away (e.g., Persephone, 1312–1313). On the ritual meaning of καλλιπάρθενοι, see Swift 2010, 222, who has shown that *Helen* is pervaded by the language and theme of parthenaic performances. On Helen's involvement in marriage rites, see Foley 2001, 308, who observes that in the cults dedicated to initiating marriageable Spartan girls, Helen eternally preserves a liminal position between the sphere of the virgins Artemis and Athena and that of the goddesses of sexuality and marriage, Aphrodite and Hera. See also Worman 2015, 15, who notes that flowing water, especially in early poetry, is sensual and relates to female rites of passages.

spectators, as they are engaged with her internal emotions via their imaginative experience of the Nile.[24]

In the second part of the prologue, Teucer, a Greek warrior returning from Troy, enters and informs Helen about the deaths of her mother, brothers, and husband. Once the man has left, Helen, alone on the stage, opens the *parodos*, abandoning herself to her grief. In the first strophe, she invites the Sirens, "winged maidens, virgin daughters of Earth" (πτεροφόροι νεάνιδες / παρθένοι Χθονὸς κόραι / Σειρῆνες, 167–169), to come from the underworld, where they figure as companions of Persephone (175), and accompany her mournful song with "the Libyan flute or the syrinxes" (Λίβυν λωτὸν ἢ σύριγγας, 171–172). Here, as Sheila Murnaghan (2013, 174) has observed, the Sirens, for whom the chorus women substitute in the next strophe, are positioned as the group of maidens from which a chosen woman is typically snatched away. In these terms, the invocation of the Sirens establishes the theme of rape and the consequent suffering as focal points of the ode by linking through mythological exempla the experience of Helen and of the chorus women to that of Persephone and the maidens.[25] This is clear in the first antistrophe, when the chorus enters in response to Helen's lament (179–190):

κυανοειδὲς ἀμφ' ὕδωρ
ἔτυχον ἕλικά τ' ἀνὰ χλόαν   180
φοίνικας ἁλίῳ
πέπλους χρυσέαισίν
‹τ' ἐν› αὐγαῖσι θάλπουσ'
ἀμφὶ δόνακος ἔρνεσιν·
ἔνθεν οἰκτρὸν ὅμαδον ἔκλυον   185
ἄλυρον ἔλεγον, ὅτι ποτ' ἔλακεν
‹λαμπροῖσιν› αἰάγμα-
σι στένουσα νύμφα τις,
οἷα Ναῒς ὄρεσι φύγδα
νόμον ἱεῖσα γοερόν, ὑπὸ δὲ
πέτρινα γύαλα κλαγγαῖσι
Πανὸς ἀναβοᾷ γάμους.   190

---

24. Zeitlin (1994, 142–143) has noted the "pervasive tendency" in Euripidean theater to emphasize the conditions and details of visual experience, either to expand the imaginative field of vision far beyond the confines of the theater or to register private emotional states. I regard the depiction of the Nile and in general of the natural environment as conjuring up a perceptual experience that prompts the spectators' sensory, cognitive, and emotional involvement in Helen's feelings.

25. For a discussion on the ode's interpretations, see Kannicht 1969, 59–94; Willink 1990; Ford 2010; Swift 2010, 222–226; Marshall 2014, 102–106; Weiss 2018.

Near dark blue water
and on the twisted grass I happened
to be drying purple robes in the sun
\<and\> its golden rays
on young reed shoots.
There I heard a piteous wail
a lyreless lament, which she uttered
in \<loud\> complaint
a nymph groaning,
just as a Naiad as she flees in the mountains
sends a woeful strain in some rocky hollows
she cries out that she is being raped by Pan.

In this impressionist description of the Nile and its surroundings, visual and aural effects are combined, as the landscape imagery intersects with the mention of the cry of the Naiad, a nymph being raped by Pan. As Weiss (2018, 150) has pointed out, by describing Helen as a Naiad the chorus reconfigure Helen as a *parthenos*, hinting at the divine abduction of a maiden.

Even natural entities as well as material things are attuned to the chorus's critique of rape. First, the Nile's waters amalgamate into the gloomy atmosphere of the ode; in fact, this time they are κυανοειδὲς ("dark blue") instead of white.[26] Next, the "purple robes" (φοίνικας πέπλους) hung on the reeds blur with the depicted gloom, as their color demarcates a dim hue of purple that is associated to κυανοειδής.[27] Finally, the golden rays of the sun contribute to the sinister significance of the chorus's words, as they recall together with the purple robes the laundry scene in the *parodos* of the *Hippolytus*, where, as Froma Zeitlin (1996, 242) has observed, "the benign heat of the sun suggests the torrid passion of eros" that provokes Phaedra's sickness. In this context, the expression ἀνὰ χλόαν ("on the grass") is also worth noting. The same expression is used in the *Hippolytus* for the "deep verdure" (βαθεῖαν ἀνὰ χλόαν, 1139) of the "untouched meadow" (ἀκήρατον / λειμῶνος, 73–74) where Hippolytus always consorts with the *parthenos* Artemis and out of which he arranges flowers for his garland to the goddess.[28]

---

26. The sinister meaning of the adjective is confirmed at line 1502, where Euripides, using the word κυανόχροα ("dark blue") for the sea swell, enhances the danger of the sea.

27. The term φοῖνιξ includes all dark reds, from crimson to purple, while the brighter shades of these colors are denoted by terms such as πορφύρεος (*LSJ*, s.v.). On the association of φοῖνιξ with κυανοειδής; see Aristotle, *Col.* 796a10–18.

28. As Zeitlin (1996, 232–233) points out, the "untouched meadow" where Hippolytus worships Artemis represents "the spatial analogue" of the young man, who defines himself as a sexually unworked territory.

In our ode, the implicit allusion to the meadow resonates with the *Hippolytus* scene and in general with the flower picking of mythological virgin girls (e.g., Europa, Persephone) or nymphs coerced by the males who intrude into their meadows.[29] In the *Helen*'s strophe, then, the highly sensorial and allusive depiction of the Nile's environment conveys feelings about female sexuality, virginal purity, and the threat of rape that jeopardizes the life of the maidens. The final mention of the Naiad, whose imaginary voice overlaps Helen's real voice on the stage, further reinforces this significance and augments the emotional appeal of the scene through sound effects.[30]

The strophe above also allows us to highlight a trans-corporeal entanglement between the chorus women as *parthenoi* and the Nile's "reeds" (δόνακος ἔρνη). In this respect, we may compare the reed stalks sustaining the robes with the bodies of the maidens draped with robes. The expression δόνακος ἔρνη (literally, "young shoots of reed") supports my argument, as it points to the relation between the delicacy of the maidens' young bodies and the delicacy of the young reed shoots.[31] The association between maidens and reeds is confirmed later in the play with the mention of the streams of the Eurotas River (ῥοαὶ / τοῦ καλλιδόνακός εἰσιν Εὐρώτα, 492–493), on whose banks the Spartan maidens celebrated parthenaic rites.[32] Here, the epithet καλλιδόναξ ("with beautiful reeds") strikingly recalls

---

29. Helen herself was abducted while picking flowers, as the last strophe of the *parodos* confirms (244–245). For a discussion on the motif of flower picking and the relation between virgin girls, meadows, rape, and female desire, see Calame 1977 and Deacy 2013.

30. The articulated description of the Naiad's cry may represent a form of "reasoning through imagery," which, in the words of Chaston (2010, 5), is a way to make a perceptual comparison between the imaginary and the real world. I suggest that here the description of the cry serves both to highlight the woeful quality of Helen's onstage lament and to render the Naiad's imagined cry vibrantly perceptible, as it were a real echo to Helen's voice. On this cry, see also Ford 2010, 295, who, by reading the rocks as the subject who shout out in accompaniment to the Naiad, interprets them as a kind of chorus in the wild that echoes the nymph's cry.

31. See Ragusa and Rosenmeyer 2019, who notes that ἔρνος ("a new palm shoot") in tragedy suggests young men and women just at the cusp of maturity. For varied examples of the use of ἔρνος in Greek literature, see Ragusa and Rosenmeyer 2019, 67 notes 31–32.

32. The relation of the maidens with the reeds would also have underscored a reference to the Caryatides, statues of maidens supporting the porch of the Erechtheion (421–406 BCE) on the Acropolis. If the Caryatides were there already in 412 BCE when the *Helen* was performed, they would have had a strong impact on the audience's reception of the depiction of the Nile's (and Eurotas's) reeds. Indeed, one version of the myth relates the Caryatides to Artemis Caryatis ("Artemis of the nut tree"), who rejoiced at the dance of the maidens "who in their ecstatic round-dance carried on their heads baskets of live reeds as they were dancing plants"; see Kerényi 1951, 149. As I show below, the relationship between statues (*agalmata*) and *parthenoi* is exploited later in the play, when Helen compares herself to an *agalma*. On "choral projection," that is, when choruses

the "lovely virgin streams" (καλλιπάρθενοι ῥοαί, 1) of the Nile, whose depiction, as mentioned above, interacts with the representation of Helen as a *parthenos*. Moreover, the two adjectives καλλιπάρθενοι and καλλιδόναξ resonate with "the lovely dancing dolphins" (τῶν καλλιχόρων / δελφίνων, 1454–1455) which surround the ship that brings Helen and the Greeks home in the third *stasimon* and which, as I show below, merge with the chorus women. It thus seems clear that in our strophe the reeds allude to parthenaic performances. In this context, it is interesting to observe that the extant *partheneia* manifest a systematic focus on visual effects that encouraged the ancient audience to notice the physical aspect of the performers and the details of their costumes, such as *peploi* or garlands made of flowers and reeds (e.g., ταὶ δὲ στεφανωσάμε[ναι φοιν]ικέων / ἀνθέων δόνακος, Bacchylides 13. 91–92).[33] The imagery of the reeds, then, renders the chorus's depictions strongly resonant to the spectators via their memory of the parthenaic performances. Finally, it is significant that in the strophe above the grass and the reeds (180, 183) are within the same musical phrase as the Libyan flute and the syrinxes in the first strophe (171, 172), as Marshall (2014, 103) has noted. This metrical correspondence allows for an interpretation of the interaction between onstage performance and descriptive space and highlights the materiality and functionality of the reeds. As a matter of fact, the Libyan flute, which was a reed instrument, evokes not only the African setting but also the *aulos* played on the stage and whose sound could have heightened the audience's engagement with the performance of the chorus members.[34]

---

look back in memory or forward in imagination to occasions of dancing outside the action of drama, see Henrichs 1996, 51.

33. Bacchylides' fragment is significant here, as both the words φοιν]ικέων and δόνακος occur in the Euripidean strophe. Swift (2016, 270–271) observes that the ancient dramatists stress visual aspects as a way of evoking *partheneia*, assuming that a mass Athenian audience not only knew about parthenaic choral song, but also that they were familiar with its distinctive features. Steiner (2021, 277) highlights the tight connection that Bacchylides 13 establishes between the internal parthenaic chorus and the performers of the composition and observes that "Even the maiden's garlands can be equated with the wreaths most likely worn by the Bacchylidean chorus."

34. Ford (2010, 288) has noted that the Sirens are to bring pipes instead of the lyres they usually bear in iconography, for lyres, which often accompanied happy songs, would not be suitable for Helen's lament (ἄλυρον ἔλεγον, 185). This reflects the general anomaly of the *parodos*, with which, as Weiss (2018, 146) has observed, Euripides highlights the novelty of his work, which revolutionized the standard structure of Athenian drama by having an actor begin the opening choral song. On the relationship between the Sirens and choral performances and on the figure of Helen as chorus leader, see below the discussion about the dancing dolphins and Calame 1977; Martin 2008, 119–126; Ford 2010; Murnaghan 2013; Weiss 2018.

II The Sirens and the Egg

I have noted above that the invocation of the Sirens as *parthenoi* serves to introduce the theme of rape, and how the Sirens are associated with the chorus women through choral performances. I turn now to the relationship between Helen and the Sirens in terms of embodiment. As stated in the Introduction, Weiss (2018, 143–150) has pointed out that a succession of "musical metamorphoses," combined with particular styles of musical performance, establishes Helen as a hybrid figure in relation to her avian heritage. Whereas this interpretation takes into account the musically hybrid nature of Helen, I read the invocation of the Sirens while focusing on the corporeal entanglement of the woman and the mythical creatures. We know from ancient literary sources, vase paintings, and sculptural figures that the Sirens were half-women and half-birds.[35] The crossbreed nature of the Sirens is strikingly relevant to Helen, as she herself was born half-woman and half-bird from Zeus's rape of her mother in the form of a swan. Euripides thus might have chosen the Sirens to highlight a trans-corporeal entanglement, as both Helen and these creatures share the same bodily hybrid nature. In this light and looking back to the *parodos*, the representation of the Sirens as virgin maidens, as companions of Persephone, becomes a poignant incarnation of Helen's innate, embodied implication with rape.

Helen's suffering thus is mediated by a human-nonhuman enmeshment embedded within her very being. This enmeshment is further exploited by the mention of the egg from which Helen was said to have been hatched. At the beginning of the first episode, while talking to the chorus women, she expresses her sorrow about her fate (255–266):

φίλαι γυναῖκες, τίνι πότμῳ συνεζύγην;   255
ἆρ' ἡ τεκοῦσά μ' ἔτεκεν ἀνθρώποις τέρας;
γυνὴ γὰρ οὔθ' Ἑλληνὶς οὔτε βάρβαρος
τεῦχος νεοσσῶν λευκὸν ἐκλοχεύεται,
ἐν ᾧ με Λήδαν φασὶν ἐκ Διὸς τεκεῖν.
τέρας γὰρ ὁ βίος καὶ τὰ πράγματ' ἐστί μου,   260
τὰ μὲν δι' Ἥραν, τὰ δὲ τὸ κάλλος αἴτιον.
εἴθ' ἐξαλειφθεῖσ' ὡς ἄγαλμ' αὖθις πάλιν

---

35. Apollonius Rhodius says that the Sirens "looked partly like birds and partly like maidens" (τότε δ' ἄλλο μὲν οἰωνοῖσιν / ἄλλο δὲ παρθενικῆς ἐναλίγκιαι ἔσκον ἰδέσθαι, *Argon.* 4.898–899). On the vase depictions and sculptural figures of the bird-women Sirens, see Tsiafakis 2001 and Padgett 2004. In our play, the visual allure and materiality of the birdlike form of the Sirens could have been enhanced by a real depiction of the Sirens on the tomb of Proteus; see Allan 2008, 171–172.

αἴσχιον εἶδος ἔλαβον ἀντὶ τοῦ καλοῦ,
καὶ τὰς τύχας μὲν τὰς κακὰς ἃς νῦν ἔχω
Ἕλληνες ἐπελάθοντο, τὰς δὲ μὴ κακὰς   265
ἔσῳζον ὥσπερ τὰς κακὰς σῴζουσί μου.

Dear women, to what fate have I been yoked?
Did my mother bear me as a monstrosity in men's eyes?
No woman, either Greek or barbarian,
ever gave birth to a white-shelled bird's egg,
yet it was in this, men say, that Leda bore me to Zeus.
My life and fortunes are a monstrosity,
partly because of Hera, partly because of my beauty.
I wish I had been wiped clean like a statue
and remade in an uglier form instead of beautiful,
and that the Greeks had forgotten the bad things that I have now
and recall the good things, just as they now remember the bad about me!

In this speech, the egg (τεῦχος νεοσσῶν λευκὸν) gives a keen sense of Helen's feeling of being a "monstrosity" (τέρας), materially illustrating her more than human nature.[36] But one other aspect of the egg emphasizes its vitality and agency: the long periphrasis used to name the egg highlights its materiality, functionality, and ontological versatility. The word τεῦχος ("eggshell") in Greek tragedy is used for a vessel of any kind—from the bathing tub in which Agamemnon falls dead in Aeschylus's *Agamemnon* (1128), to the empty urn of Orestes in Sophocles' *Electra* (1114), to the cup full of the poisoned wine offered to Ion in Euripides' *Ion* (1184). In line with these objects, the egg metaphorically encapsulates the tragic sense of Helen's experience, but while it serves as a metaphor for Helen's sorrowful feelings, it also possesses a vitality on its own, drawing the audience into dynamic modes of engagement with Helen's emotional experience. Seen in the light of what Jane Bennett (2010, 6) calls "thing-power," the egg shows "the curious ability of inanimate things to animate, to act, to produce effects dramatic and subtle." This ability is foregrounded by the νεοσσοί ("little chicks") which engender a high degree of humanity to the egg; in fact, the word νεοσσός is often used, especially in Euripides, of young children to evoke pity on their behalf (*Alc.* 403; *Heracl.* 239; *Andr.* 441). We may consider then the egg an assemblage that includes both human and nonhuman qualities that are ultimately embodied by Helen herself, as she hatched

---

36. Helen was so inextricably linked to the egg that it is with it that she was worshipped in cults and was often represented in vase paintings. On the association between Helen and the egg in cults and vase paintings, see Blondell 2013, 28–47.

out from the egg like a little chick. This entanglement between Helen and the chicks enables the woman to further arouse the spectators' sympathy for her story.

But the egg is also a bizarre thing that denotes a jarring and estranging sense of monstrosity and hints at comic effects. Its "white color" (λευκόν) is remarkable in this regard, placing the egg against another dramatic egg, namely, in Aristophanes' *Birds* the "black-winged egg" (μελανόπτερος ᾠόν, 695) which the Night lays and from which Eros hatches out with "his golden wings" (πτερύγοιν χρυσαῖν, 697). It may be possible that Euripides intended an oblique reference to the Aristophanic cosmological egg birth, in order to challenge the audience's expectations about Helen's story.[37] In this context, we may observe that in Aristophanes all the birds originate from Eros: they indeed have wings and lend assistance to the lovers (*Av.* 705). A representation of Helen's avian nature in terms that emphasize love is deployed later in the play when Euripides describes the woman's excitement for her reunion with Menelaus. Here, by means of a cross-embodiment, Helen's "hair," or better "feathers," raise upright on her head" (κρατὶ δ' ὀρθίους ἐθείρας / ἀνεπτέρωσα, 632–633), vividly manifesting her happiness. This birdlike representation of Helen reverses the poignancy of her relationship with the Sirens and contributes to exploiting the tragicomic nuances of the play.

III The *Agalma* and the Mask

In the passage above, another nonhuman entity that signifies Helen's feelings and mingles her sense of monstrosity with her sense of guilt for the Trojan War is the ἄγαλμα ("statue"). At 262–266, Helen bewails her beauty, wishing that she had been "wiped clean like an *agalma*" (εἴθ' ἐξαλειφθεῖσ' ὡς ἄγαλμα), so that she could be painted "once again" (αὖθις πάλιν) to get an "uglier form" (αἴσχιον εἶδος).[38] In these lines, it seems clear that the *agalma* substitutes for Helen's body;

---

37. Regarding the white color of the Nile's waters, in *Thes.* 855–857 Aristophanes parodies Euripides' depiction of the Nile by quoting the entire initial three lines of *Helen*'s prologue. He only changes the last line, where he says that the Nile's waters flood the fields of "white" (λευκῆς) Egypt and produce the "black syrmea" (μελανοσυρμαῖον) for a people much given to laxatives. The wordplay on the colors white and black may be a subtle clue interrelating the Nile and the egg in response to Euripides' depiction. The close dates of the *Birds* (c. 414–413 BCE), *Helen* (412 BCE), and *Thesmophoriazusae* (411 BCE) would make the parody strongly effective for the audience.

38. Allan (2008, 180) has commented on the difficulty in choosing between the two senses of ἄγαλμα ("statue" or "painting") because in ancient sculpture paint was applied also to statues and so they, like pictures, could be "wiped clean." The reference to the painting seems to relate to the *Agamemnon* in which Aeschylus describes the destruction of a picture with a wet sponge (*Ag.* 1327–1330). Steiner (2001, 55) has insisted upon the statue, noting that the formula of the painted *agalma* presupposes a painted figure in the round, whose surface could be changed while the underlying person remained the same. I agree with Steiner, as the process of wiping may be put in

hence, her desire to be relieved of her shameful reputation coincides with "wiping clean" (ἐξαλείφω) the statue, which, as a result, would be plain and thus uglier.[39] Beyond this technical connotation, I would urge a greater recognition of the cognitive meaning of the verb ἐξαλείφω, that is, "wiping out something from one's mind." This meaning occurs in Euripides' *Hecuba*, where the woman says that she is "unable to efface from her mind" (οὐκ ἂν δυναίμην ἐξαλείψασθαι φρενός, 590) the memory of the sacrifice of her daughter Polyxena, whose "breasts and bosom" are compared to those of an *agalma* (μαστούς τ' ἔδειξε στέρνα θ' ὡς ἀγάλματος / κάλλιστα, 560–561).[40] Here the verb is affectively laden, allowing us to argue that in the *Helen* the reference to the *agalma* has a multimodal aesthetic, cognitive, and emotional appeal that renders Helen's attitude and feelings towards her beauty vividly perceptible for the audience.[41]

As the *Hecuba*'s passage shows, the *agalma* embodies young virgin girls, and in our play it is an integral part of the patterning that relates Helen to the *parthenoi*. Ruth Scodel (1996) has observed that in Greek tragedy the *agalma* imagery reflects the actual social function of the maidens, whose comparison to ornaments was related to their preparation for marriage. This use is underscored in two moments of the play: when Helen calls Proteus's daughter, Eido, her mother's "delight" (ἀγλάϊσμα, 11), and when she defines her own daughter, Hermione, "her house's delight" (ἀγλάϊσμα δωμάτων, 282).[42] These examples make clear that the *agalma*

---

relation with the ancient technical process called *ganōsis*, the process of applying plaster or wax to tone down the glare of the marble, especially of statues, which then was rubbed down with clean cloths. The primary sources for this practice are Pliny (*NH* 33.122), Plutarch (*QR* 287), and Vitruvius (7.9.3–4). See also Zeitlin 1981, 324, and 2010, 274, where she notes that Helen senses herself as an "*objet d'art*, a source of aesthetic wonder that counters the uncanny quality of the supernatural *eidōlon* in the archaic sense with the technical properties of an artist's mimetic skill."

39. As Gaifman and Platt (2018) observe, in Greek culture *agalmata* ("delightful objects") were associated with the archaic category of *korai*, statues of maidens that displayed bright colors. Stieber (2011, 176) observes that a fifth-century audience thoroughly familiar with the practice of polychromy would retain a mental picture of the "before and after" appearance of the typical white marble statue, even if there were no real-life occasion for the removal of polychromy, as is likely.

40. It may also be relevant that Plato uses ἐξαλείφω (ἐξαλείψομεν ἄρα) in *Republic* 386C to refer to the kind of poetry that should be "wiped out" in Kallipolis. Thus, the verb may also underscore a metapoetic significance, pointing up Helen's wish that the spectators forget the traditional Iliadic narrative, in which she and her beauty are responsible for the Trojan War. On Polyxena's statue and scene, see Stieber 2011, 147–153.

41. In regard to the audience's engagement with artefacts, see Gaifman and Platt 2018, 412, who consider *agalmata* as "embodied objects" that assume and interact with the human bodies, "challenging conventional distinctions between inert artefact and their sentient audience."

42. On the close association in the play of the two words ἀγλάϊσμα with ἄγαλμα, see Downing 1990, 4. In this context, the meaning of Eido ("beauty" or "appearance") is intriguing, in that it underlines the aesthetic role of the maidens' appearance.

reinforces the charged relationship between Helen and the maidens. But I want to draw attention to one further point. Blondell (2013, 209) has noted that through the image of the *agalma*, Helen presents herself as a "transformed Pandora," a woman whose beautiful exterior hides a virtuous character.[43] I want to discuss how the association of the *agalma* with mythical women is useful for assessing Helen's condition of wife, especially the faithful wife.[44]

As already mentioned, Helen is traditionally associated with statues. As a matter of fact, Aeschylus in *Agamemnon* reveals that the beautiful statues (εὐμόρφων δὲ κολοσσῶν, 416) of Helen in her palace became the object of Menelaus's loathing for his absent wife. I posit that Euripides reacts against the Aeschylean representation by making the *agalma* an agent of Helen's moral redemption. A good comparandum is Alcestis, "the best of women [or wives]" (ἀρίστη γυνή, 151), who in Euripides' play *Alcestis* is, like Helen, associated with a statue and experiences a renewed marriage with her husband. In the play, Admetus promises Alcestis, who accepts to die in his place, that he will keep her "statue" shaped by the "skilled hand of craftsmen" (σοφῇ δὲ χειρὶ τεκτόνων δέμας τὸ σόν, 348) in his bed as a consolation for his mourning life. Admetus's promise foregrounds a notion of equivalence between Alcestis's body and its manufactured figure, the result being that the statue takes the place of his wife.[45] This notion reaches a further complexity in the *Helen*: an affective transaction between Helen and the statue, which in the *Alcestis* is mediated by Admetus. This could explain the different terms used for the statue: δέμας in the *Alcestis* and ἄγαλμα in the *Helen*. The word δέμας reflects Admetus's desire of having his wife alive, which is ultimately realized at the end of the play when Alcestis returns to life and Admetus uses the same

---

43. See also Worman 1997, 158–160, who has observed that Helen's body represents "the exemplary object of male desire"; for instance, in *Iliad* 3 it is measured against possessions, such as an ornate tapestry, a golden suit for arms, or a bronze bowl, objects that were often given in gift exchange, or snatched in the plundering of cities.

44. Helen is represented both as a maiden and as a wife. The suggestion of this hybridity through the figure of Persephone in the *parodos*, as Weiss (2018, 152) notes, points to Helen's metamorphosis from the one to the other following the arrival of Menelaus. I think that the *agalma* represents an important element of connection between the two phases and anticipates the representation of Helen as a faithful wife.

45. Scholars have compared Admetus's experience to that of Laodamia, who had a bronze image made of her husband Protesilaus and placed it in her bed. As this proved to be poor comfort, Laodamia asked the god to let Protesilaus visit her by inhabiting the statue. This episode constitutes the theme of the Euripidean *Protesilaus*, where Laodamia is caught in bed with the statue of her dead husband. See esp. fr. 655 N2: οὐκ ἂν προδοίην καίπερ ἄψυχον φίλον ("I shall not forsake a loved one, even though he is lifeless"). Pointing out that Admetus, presumably, applies his hands (χέρας, 350) to the imagined statue, Stieber (1999, 156–157) has underlined the "sexual innuendo" of Admetus's vision.

word δέμας to refer to her body (1133–1134).⁴⁶ Instead, the *agalma* underscores the centrality of Helen's beauty, externalizing her embodied, personal feelings that mesh up with the materiality of the statue itself. Helen's desire to erase her beauty by wiping clean the *agalma*, accordingly, spurs the audience to clearly perceive the anguish that her beauty brings her.⁴⁷

The *agalma* highlights Helen's virtue by showing her willingness to save the Greeks and her ability to persuade people about her good intentions. Once Helen has left the stage, Menelaus enters. Coming from Troy, he has been shipwrecked in Egypt and now he seeks hospitality. He meets Helen, and after recognizing each other they are reconciled, while the *eidōlon* disappears by vanishing in the air (605–607). Reunited, the two plan their escape from Egypt. Helen assumes an active role in the planning, saying that she will convince Theoclymenus to give a ship to the Greeks to return home. As a strategy she proposes to perform a fake burial rite for her husband, leading Theoclymenus to believe that Menelaus is dead. The rite will happen by the sea, so that Helen will have the opportunity to embark on the ship and flee with the Greeks. According to the plan, Helen will enter the palace to prepare herself for the rite. As she tells the audience, she will cut her hair, change her clothing from white to black, and "scratch her cheeks until they bloody her skin" (παρῇδί τ' ὄνυχα φόνιον ἐμβαλῶ χροός, 1089)—all signifiers of mourning and typical of bereaved women (e.g., the Trojan mourners 367–374). Nevertheless, in the context of the performance, these acts combined with the actor's change of the mask and/or costume. We may say then that Helen's changed mask becomes the onstage counterpart of the *agalma*, giving a concrete weight to her rejection of her beauty. Indeed, the scratched cheeks and bloodied skin materialize the defacement that Helen has imagined for the *agalma*.⁴⁸

---

46. Scholars still debate on the exact meaning of δέμας. Bassi (2018, 46–47) has pointed out that while Admetus says that Alcestis's body's likeness is to be fashioned by craftsmen, he does not explicitly refer to it as a statue or ἄγαλμα. Rather, as she observes, this likeness is rendered ambiguous by the fact that δέμας emphasizes the double nature of Alcestis as both alive and dead. I think that the reference to the craftsmen's hands that skillfully shape the bodily figure is powerful at a cognitive level: it fosters the spectators' imagination of a statue that is almost a living body, in relation to the lifelike powers attributed to statues and *eidōla* in Greek mythology (Blondell 2013, 220). Therefore, for the scene to work for the audience at the end of the play, δέμας points up the sensory allure of Alcestis's body and its affective impact on Admetus, who realizes that his dream has come true.

47. As Chaniotis (2017) observes, ancient Greek statues both represent emotional experience and elicit emotional responses in the audiences. See also Day 2010, 125, who has shown that in archaic Greek dedicatory epigrams *agalma* connoted "an ornament that generates friendly responses with its beauty."

48. Hall (2006, 103) associates Helen's *agalma* to the mask and its manufacture: "The face painted on the dried rags-plaster laminate, once dried and removed from the mould, could vary in

The mask plays a consistent role in Helen's deception of Theoclymenus. The king's reaction to Helen's look is significant in that it helps us to emphasize the materiality, vitality, and allure of the mask. When he sees Helen, Theoclymenus asks why she is in a mourning guise (1186–1190):

αὕτη, τί πέπλους μέλανας ἐξήψω χροὸς
λευκῶν ἀμείψασ' ἔκ τε κρατὸς εὐγενοῦς
κόμας σίδηρον ἐμβαλοῦσ' ἀπέθρισας
χλωροῖς τε τέγγεις δάκρυσι σὴν παρηίδα
κλαίουσα;   1190

You, why do you fasten black robes to your skin,
changed from white? Why from your noble head
have you taken steel and cut your hair?
Why do you wet your cheeks with fresh tears
and cry?

In this passage, the king calls attention to the cropped hair and black clothing, and refers to Helen's cheeks as "wet" (τέγγεις) with "fresh tears" (χλωροῖς δάκρυσι). The adjective χλωρός and the present tense of the verb τέγγω are remarkable here, implying the immediate occurrence of weeping (e.g., the tears trickling down Helen's cheeks/mask). In the play χλωρός is used elsewhere twice: for the Eurotas River, which is "fecund with water reeds" (τὸν ὑδρόεντι δόνακι χλωρὸν, 349) and for the "fresh petals of roses" (χλοερὰ / ῥόδεα πέταλα, 244–245) which Helen collects in her robes when abducted by Hermes. By foregrounding a blurring of natural and human characteristics, both references evoke fertilizing wetness and flourishing richness as particularly suitable for the freshness and abundance of Helen's tears.[49] We are not able to say, however, whether the tears were flooding the Helen actor's eyes or were an integral part of the mask.[50] But it seems clear that Helen's tears have a strong impact on Theoclymenus, as evidenced by the use of

---

appearance—as Helen says in Euripides' *Helen*, you could wipe the paint off a beautiful inanimate visage and replace it with paint depicting ugly features." For an overview on the manufacture, function, and aesthetics of the Greek tragic mask, see Halliwell 1993, 195–211; Hall 2006, 99–140; Wiles 2007, 6; Powers 2014, 99–115.

49. On the use of χλωρός for tears, see Mastronarde 2002, 317. Commenting on the chorus's tears (χλωρὸν [...] δάκρυ) at *Medea* 906, he points out that the adjective implies a visual suggestion, either of "glistening" surface or the "swelling" shape of droplets. For a discussion on the meaning of χλωρός in Greek literature, see Irwin 1974, 31–78; Clarke 2004, 13; Clements 2016.

50. As Wiles (2007, 222) has noted, faces in tragedy were not stable, with many references in tragedy to masked faces that supposedly wept. See Wiles 222 note 56 for references.

τέγγω, which occurs in other Euripidean plays. For example, in the *Alcestis*, the hapax ὀφθαλμότεγκτος ("wet eye") indicates the flood of Alcestis's tears that drench all her bed (πᾶν δὲ δέμνιον / ὀφθαλμοτέγκτῳ δεύεται πλημμυρίδι, 183–184). In the *parodos* of the *Hippolytus*, τέγγω describes the wetting of the royal purple garments in the water river by the chorus women (πορφύρεα φάρεα / ποταμίᾳ δρόσῳ / τέγγουσα, 126–128). The wetting of the garments finds its analogue in the tears that the chorus women shed for the misfortunes of the royal house (δάκρυσί μου βλέφαρα / καταχυθέντα τέγγεται σᾷ τύχαι, 853–854). Finally, in the *Suppliants*, the verb describes the chorus women's tears that wet the folds of their robes (δάκρυσι νοτερὸν ἀεὶ πέπλων πρὸς στέρνῳ πτύχα τέγξω, 978–979). In these plays, τέγγω demarcates a charged relationship between garments, female embodiment, and expression of feelings. Indeed, as Zeitlin (1996, 242) has observed in relation to the *Hippolytus*'s scenes, "Like the clothing they soften in the water, women are expected to be pliant and permeable themselves." These examples help show a correspondence between the garments and Helen's mask, whose common denominator lies in their wet fabric, and this in its own turn blends with human, embodied feelings of grief. Within this context, the pliant mask also takes on an active performative role, as it sharpens Helen's ability to arouse Theoclymenus's pity. This network of intra-actions between Helen and the mask engenders the successful outcome of the king's deception.

IV The Shrouds and the Ship

In tears, Helen tells Theoclymenus about Menelaus's death, which, as she says, was reported by the Greek man (Menelaus) sitting at Proteus's tomb (ὅδ᾽ ὃς κάθηται τῷδ᾽ ὑποπτήξας τάφῳ, 1203). Taking advantage of Theoclymenus's pity, Helen convinces him to give the Greeks a ship and then tells him that before sending them home, she wants to perform a burial rite for her missing husband. In this section, I concentrate on the shrouds that Helen uses for Menelaus's burial and on the Phoenician ship that the king gives to the Greeks. My intent is to show that the two things connect to Helen through a mutual constitution of intra-actions.

The aim of the fake burial rite is to honor Menelaus's memory in the Greek custom (1239). As Helen says, when a man dies at the sea the Greeks buried his absent body "in empty shrouds" (κενοῖσι ἐν πέπλων ὑφάσμασιν, 1243).[51] The πέπλων ὑφάσματα ("woven robes") recall Helen's traditional association with robes, especially the "great web" (μέγαν ἱστὸν) into which she "weaved" (ὕφαινε) the story of the Trojan War at *Iliad* 3.125–128 and the "richly embroidered robes"

---

51. Menelaus's empty tomb and shrouds would evoke the empty biers used in Athenian state funerals for the fallen men whose bodies were not recovered; see Allan 2008, 289.

(οἱ πέπλοι παμποίκιλοι) which she offered as a gift to Telemachus at *Odyssey* 15.105–129. These references allow us to see that the πέπλων ὑφάσματα in our play allude to Helen's care of the household; in fact, in the *Odyssey* weaving aligns Helen to Penelope as a symbol of their common effort to support the *oikos*.[52] However, ὑφάσματα resonates with a famous tragic robe, namely, the "spider's web" (ἀράχνης ἐν ὑφάσματι) made by Clytemnestra's hands and in which Agamemnon laid dead at *Agamemnon* 1492.[53] This allusion, together with the Homeric references, open up memories and feelings about Helen's story through which the spectators would have regarded her deceptive action in a fresh light: aiming at saving her husband instead of killing him.[54]

The shrouds therefore give a concrete weight to the good deeds (τὰς δὲ μὴ κακὰς, 265) which Helen wished to achieve when she mentioned the *agalma*. But the shrouds have a further quality that complicates our interpretation: they are empty. In the play, the adjective κενός ("empty") is used not only for the shrouds but also for Menelaus's "empty tomb" (κενῷ τάφῳ, 1057) to which Helen refers when she explains her strategic plan to her husband. Weiberg (2020, 747) has regarded the empty tomb as part of a discourse of material signs, known only by Helen and Menelaus, which reinforces their union. Weiberg does not include the empty shrouds among the symbolic terms of the couple's reunion, but I think they play a central role in showing Helen's support of her marriage to Menelaus and, by implication, to the audience. If we approach the empty shrouds from a perspective that emphasizes their materiality, and more specifically the elaborate quality of their textile, we may say that they acquire a strong allure and incorporate Helen's intricate scheme of deception. These characteristics show that Helen's and the empty shrouds' agencies are utterly imbricated, such that they form an alliance, so to speak, to deceive Theoclymenus, thereby assuring Menelaus's survival.

Helen's association with robes is implicitly foregrounded in the third *stasimon* through the depiction of the ship that Theoclymenus gives to the Greeks. In this ode, the chorus sings of Helen and Menelaus's happy return home (1451–1511). As

---

52. On the relationship between Helen and Penelope and their common care of the household by means of the robes and weaving, see Canevaro 2018, 55–97, and Stockdale 2020, 8–9. On Helen and weaving in the *Odyssey*, see also Mueller 2010.

53. For a discussion on the *Agamemnon*'s tapestry, see Mueller 2016, 42–69, who demonstrates how the more immediate causes of Agamemnon's capitulation are to be found in the tapestry's "overpowering visual and sensory output, qualities that it possesses by virtues of its elaborate pattern-weave and distinctive purple dye."

54. Worman (1999, 35), discussing Helen's gift of her woven robes to Telemachus in *Odyssey* 15.107–129, suggests that the heroine exercises an impressive control over the signification of the object, "transforming it from a would-be ruinous object into one with happy associations." My focus is on the vital materiality of the shrouds, as they contribute to Helen's successful action.

Marshall (2014, 122–123) has pointed out, the ode helps to define the structure of the play by pulling together a variety of images and themes that have been present throughout the play.[55] The depiction of the ship is illuminating, especially regarding Helen's story of rape and her virtuous behavior. The ship appears in the first strophe (1451–1464):

> Φοίνισσα Σιδωνιὰς ὦ
> ταχεῖα κώπα, ῥοθίοισι Νηρέως
> εἰρεσία φίλα,
> χοραγὲ τῶν καλλιχόρων
> δελφίνων, ὅταν αὐ-   1455
> ρᾶν πέλαγος ἀνήνεμον ᾖ,
> γλαυκὰ δὲ Πόντου θυγάτηρ
> Γαλάνεια τάδ' εἴπῃ·
> Κατὰ μὲν ἱστία πετάσετ', αὔ-
> ρας πλέοντες εἰναλίας,   1460
> λάβετε δ' εἰλατίνας πλάτας,
> ὦ ναῦται ‹ἴτε› ναῦται,
> πέμποντες εὐλιμένους
> Περσείων οἴκων Ἑλέναν ἐπ' ἀκτάς.

> O swift Phoenician ship of Sidon,
> oarage, dear to Nereus's waves,
> leader of the lovely dancing
> dolphins whenever the
> sea is calm and windless
> and the gray-eyed daughter of Pontus
> Galeneia says these words:
> "Spread the sails leaving
> the sea breezes behind,
> and take up your fir wood oars,
> O sailors, <go> sailors,
> escorting Helen to the well-harbored shores of Perseus's home."

The depiction of the Phoenician ship and its surrounding landscape introduces Helen's return to Greece. The ship is distinct from the other ships earlier in the play, the "barbarian ships" (βαρβάρου πλάτας, 191) which transported to Egypt the

---

55. On the ode's pertinence to the larger structure and themes of the play, see also Padel 1974, 235–240.

Greek women as "captives" (literally, "spoils" [θήραμα, 191]), the "ruinous ship" (ὀλόμενον σκάφος, 232) which brought Paris to Helen and thus caused tears for Ilion (τὰν δακρυόεσσαν / Ἰλίῳ πεύκαν, 230–231), and Menelaus's ship, smashed in countless pieces (πολλοὺς ἀριθμοὺς ἄγνυται ναυαγίων, 410) and whose "cast-offs" (ναὸς ἔκβολα, 422) have served as the hero's rags.[56] The Phoenician ship swiftly escorts Helen home, propelled by sea breezes and surrounded by dancing dolphins (καλλιχόρων δελφίνων). By associating the dolphins' dancing motion with choral dances, scholars have interpreted the ship as a metaphor for the "chorus leader" (χορηγός), according to Helen's traditional leadership of parthenaic performances.[57]

The ship, then, functions as a metaphorical image for choral activities, but it also operates as a material symbol and an embodied object that incorporates Helen's past suffering and reformed virtue. An analysis of the terms "Phoenician" (Φοίνισσα) and "Sidonian" (Σιδωνιάς) proves this charged relationship between Helen and the ship. Φοίνισσα, in addition to being a geographical appellative, is the feminine of φοῖνιξ ("purple"), which, as we saw of the *parodos*, describes the robes (φοίνικας πέπλους, 6.181–182) which the chorus women hang on the reeds.[58] Phoenician or Sidonian skills in textile work are celebrated in *Iliad* 6. While sailing with Helen, Paris receives at Sidon robes richly embroidered by the Sidonian women (οἱ πέπλοι παμποίκιλα ἔργα γυναικῶν / Σιδονίων), which he

---

56. The majority of scholars have read Menelaus's rags as part of Euripides' response to Aristophanes' parody. For a bibliography, see Mureddu 2003; Marshall 2014, 33; Zuckerberg 2016, 207. I consider the rags from a materialist perspective as part of the entanglement between the ship and Menelaus's body. Indeed, whether with comic effect or not, the depiction of the rags as "cast-offs of the ship" sets up the verbal metaphor as a corporeal one, as if Menelaus were clothed in his own shipwreck. The use of ποικίλος ("embroidered"), which is often used for robes, for the ship's parts (ποικίλων ἁρμοσμάτων, 411) confirms this interpretation. From the viewpoint of this entanglement, the image of the ship shattered into pieces would materialize Menelaus's lost heroic identity, which he regains through the new armor obtained for him by Helen from Theoclymenus.

57. See Allan 2008, 320; Swift 2010, 227–229; Steiner 2011; Marshall 2014, 131–132; Weiss 2018, 180–189. Steiner (2021, 331–332) considers the scene of the dancing dolphins in relation to the spectacle currently presented to the theater audience, where the chorus members would dance to the music supplied by the piper. As she says, "the *auletēs* would assume the role of the *triēraculēs*, whose piping served to set the rhythm for the oarsmen." Thus, just as the dolphins leap to the beat of the rowers, so the chorus dance to the music of the piper. Steiner's interpretation highlights the conflation between the chorus's performance and the maritime landscape, which in its own turn supports my interpretation of the chorus women's identification with the reeds and of the correlated playing of the piper in the *parodos*.

58. The term φοῖνιξ is related to the fact that the Phoenicians discovered and first used this color (e.g., Homer, *Il.* 4.141, 6.219).

then takes to Troy (*Il.* 6. 289–292).⁵⁹ Following Homer but giving a different version of the story, Herodotus reveals that Helen and Paris during their voyage to Troy were driven by a storm to Egypt, where Helen and her "wealth" (χρήματα), possibly including the Sidonian robes, remained, while King Proteus sent Paris to Troy (2.113–116).⁶⁰ I wonder whether Euripides might have put these two versions into dialogue with each other, so that the terms "Phoenician" and "Sidonian" in the strophe above would not only indicate the geographical origin of the ship but also allude to the story of Helen's rape. The word Sidonian further reinforces the interconnection between Helen, ship, rape, and robes, as it is a reminiscence of the "Sidonian veils" (Σιδονίαι καλύπτραι) which the Danaids tear to shreds in Aeschylus's *Suppliants* 120–121.⁶¹ The Danaids were virgin maidens who escaped from Egypt to Argo in Greece to protect themselves from marriage to their abusive cousins, and their story intersects with the tale of Helen and the chorus women, who are maidens under the threat of rape. However, Euripides reacts against the Aeschylean representation; in fact, whereas the Danaids tear their Sidonian veils to shreds, in our strophe the chorus highlight the excellence and integrity of the Sidonian ship.⁶² In these terms, the Phoenician ship of Sidon, we may say, interacts with and substitutes for Helen, incorporating in its materiality her suffering for rape and ultimately her virtuous integrity.

Through their entanglement Helen and the ship share a striking degree of agency and become co-leaders of the Greeks' successful return home.⁶³ This collaboration

---

59. In the Iliadic passage, Hecuba had the Sidonian robes but was urged by Hector to offer them to the temple of Athena in order to save Troy (*Il.* 6.288–296).

60. For a discussion on the two Homeric and Herodotean versions, see Ford 2002, 149.

61. As Sommerstein (2019, 128–129) notes, the ethnicon Σιδόνιος in Aeschylus underscores the fact that the Danaids' veils were finely made and expensive.

62. On the excellence of Sidonian ships, see Herodotus 7.96.1: τούτων δὲ ἄριστα πλεούσας παρείχοντο νέας Φοίνικες καὶ Φοινίκων Σιδώνιοι ("Of these [Persian, Mede, and Sacae ships], the most seaworthy were furnished by the Phoenicians and among them by the Sidonian").

63. Because of the recent destruction of the Athenian fleet in the Sicilian expedition, the entanglement of the ship's excellence and Helen's moral integrity would have carried a special emotional weight for the contemporary audience, as they both contribute to the Greeks' successful return home in the play. The Sicilian expedition took place from 415–413 BCE during the Peloponnesian War, and *Helen* was performed in Athens in 412 BCE. For an account of the devastating Sicilian expedition, see Thucydides Books 6–7. Scholars (e.g., Allan 2008, 4–9) have abundantly commented on the relationship of the *Helen* to the Peloponnesian War and especially the Sicilian Expedition. Allan contradicts the positions of those critics who have argued that the *Helen* reflects the disillusionment of "a war-wearied generation," observing that such a notion is misguided and anachronistic. I see the focus on ships as a trait that helps us to contextualize the play's relationship with the war and thus refine our understanding of the spectators' emotional involvement in the dramatic action.

is foregrounded in the messenger's speech that describes the ship's launch amid the fight between Theoclymenus's men and the Greeks (1531–1536):

Σιδωνίαν ναῦν πρωτόπλουν καθείλκομεν
ζυγῶν τε πεντήκοντα κἀρετμῶν μέτρα
ἔχουσαν. ἔργου δ' ἔργον ἐξημείβετο·
ὁ μὲν γὰρ ἱστόν, ὁ δὲ πλάτην καθίστατο
†ταρσόν τε χειρὶ† λευκά θ' ἱστί' †εἰς ἓν ἦν† 1535
πηδάλιά τε ζεύγλαισι παρακαθίετο.

We launched a new (making its first voyage) Sidonian ship
With rooms for fifty rowing benches and
oars. And now one task followed another.
One man puts on board the mast, and another the oars;
the white sails were put in place, and
the rudders were lowered into the sea by ropes.

This description puts the ship and its parts (benches, oars, mast, sails, rudders) on prominent display. The human work on the ship represents an animating force that complements its functionality, such that the vehicle's fittingness vibrantly comes to the surface. At this point, Theoclymenus's men realize the trick and begin fighting with the Greeks (1600–1612):

ὀρθοὶ δ' ἀνῇξαν πάντες, οἱ μὲν ἐν χεροῖν 1600
κορμοὺς ἔχοντες ναυτικούς, οἱ δὲ ξίφη·
φόνῳ δὲ ναῦς ἐρρεῖτο. παρακέλευσμα δ' ἦν
πρύμνηθεν Ἑλένης· Ποῦ τὸ Τρωϊκὸν κλέος;
δείξατε πρὸς ἄνδρας βαρβάρους. σπουδῆς δ' ὕπο
ἔπιπτον, οἱ δ' ὠρθοῦντο, τοὺς δὲ κειμένους 1605
νεκροὺς ἂν εἶδες. Μενέλεως δ' ἔχων ὅπλα,
ὅπῃ νοσοῖεν ξύμμαχοι κατασκοπῶν,
ταύτῃ προσῇγε χειρὶ δεξιᾷ ξίφος,
ὥστ' ἐκκολυμβᾶν ναός· ἠρήμωσε δὲ
σῶν ναυβατῶν ἐρέτμ'· ἐπ' οἰάκων δὲ βὰς 1610
ἄνακτ' ἐς Ἑλλάδ' εἶπεν εὐθύνειν δόρυ.
οἱ δ' ἱστὸν ᾖραν, οὔριαι δ' ἧκον πνοαί.

Everyone stood up, some holding oars,
others with swords in their hands.
The ship was flowing with blood. Helen from the stern

urged them on: "Where is your Trojan glory?
Show it off to these barbarians!" In the hard fight
some men fell down, others you saw
lying dead. Menelaus, clothed in armor,
whenever he saw his friends in trouble, there he was
brandishing his sword in his right hand,
<putting all his adversaries to flight>
so that they (the rowers) leapt into the water from the ship:
and he cleared the benches of your rowers. Going to the steersman
he ordered him to make for Greece.
His men raised the mast, and the winds blew favorable.

In this passage, the entanglement between human body parts and pieces of the ship reaches its apotheosis, such that oars, swords, and hands become active agents that equally drive the fight forward. The image of the ship "flowing with blood" (φόνῳ δὲ ναῦς ἐρρεῖτο) is powerful in the terms of this human-nonhuman entanglement. The word φόνος ("blood") highlights the visual allure of the gore that has been shed as a result of the violence, while the image of the ship flowing (ἐρρεῖτο) with blood gives a keen sense of the vehicle's enmeshment with the massacre of men. The flow of the blood resonates with the "flowing streams" (ῥοαί, 1) of the Nile, rapturing the initial harmony between the Egyptian land and Helen. Here, indeed, Helen becomes the leader of the battle, as she encourages the Greek men to fight. Finally, in a mutual, bodily interplay, while Helen stands on the stern of the ship, the mast is raised up.[64] This image vividly conveys the collaborative action of Helen and the ship in leading the Greek men home.

V Helen Island and the End of the Play

The battle scene emphasizes the violence of warfare, which comes to an end with the intervention of the Dioscuri *ex machina*. After ordering Theoclymenus to restrain his rage and let Helen return with her husband (1642–1661), Castor turns to her sister and tells her that she shall sail on with favoring breeze (πλεῖ ξὺν πόσει σῷ· πνεῦμα δ' ἕξετ' οὔριον, 1663). The winds will escort Helen and the Greeks home, while the Dioscuri will ride over the sea (πόντον παριππεύοντε,

---

64. The references to the ship's mast might have resonated with the architectonical space of the Acropolis and in particular with the Odeon, which was built next to the Theater of Dionysus between 446 and 442 BCE to celebrate the defeat of the Persian fleet in the battle of Salamis. Its shape, and in particular its roof, was said to have been modelled to recall the war tent of Xerxes, while the pillars and beams within it incorporated the masts of the Persian ships; see Beacham 2007, 208.

1665) beside the ship. This speech allows the spectators to visualize the Sidonian ship in a jovial marine landscape that gives a vivid sense of the play's happy ending. Next, Castor predicts that after her death Helen will be called a goddess and that "the island stretched along the Attic coast as a guard" (φρουρὸν παρ' Ἀκτὴν τεταμένην νῆσον λέγω, 1673) and where Hermes stole her body will bear her name (Ἑλένη, 1674).[65] The *aition* of the island projects Helen's story into a cultic sphere, which links the mythical past to the present time. One could argue that in becoming forever associated with the island where she was abducted, Helen may experience a form of alienation, instead of reintegration into the Greek society. However, the island stands for not only Helen's abduction but also her deification, as here the Greeks will worship her as a goddess. As Phiroze Vasunia (2001, 39), citing Foley, has observed, "Tragedy ultimately cannot tolerate female empowerment," and so Helen's fame is "relegated to her cult by the Dioscuri." In accordance with the role of the other nonhuman beings in the play, the island is a material entity that is strongly entangled with Helen's personal story. Furthermore, in the traumatic time of the performance that followed the disastrous expedition to Sicily, the reference to the island must have had a deep emotional impact on the spectators.

As a topographical symbol, the island signifies Helen's experience of abduction and return in relation to the play's discourse of her association with Persephone. Whereas some scholars have viewed Helen's return from Egypt as cognate with Persephone's return from Hades, others have posited that this association does not exist, since in the play nothing suggests that Persephone returns from the Underworld.[66] In this respect, Heather Sebo (2014, 147) argues that Euripides uses Persephone's story—especially in the choral odes (e.g., the depiction of famine in the second *stasimon* caused by Demeter's anger)—to accentuate a vision of catastrophe inherent in the human condition. None of these interpretations, however, focus on Helen Island, perhaps because it seems a typical use of etiology at the end of the play. Francis Dunn, indeed, has pointed out (1996, 136–147) that the *aition* is simply part of the Euripidean "avant-garde conventionality," which surprises the audience with a gratuitous manner of reaching the happy end. But I would offer a different explanation of the presence of the island at the finale and of its charged relationship with Helen: Why does Euripides choose a Greek island for Helen's deification? One would think that Euripides would have linked the *aition* of the island to the myth of Persephone, who was abducted by Hades on an island, either

---

65. See Allan 2008, 34, who notes that the island called Helen (now Makronissos) lies off the southeast coast of Attica. By referring to Castor's words at 1673, he contradicts Duchemin 1940, who suggests that the island was located off Egypt.

66. For a discussion on the scholars' different views, see Foley 2001, 301–332, and Sebo 2014.

Crete or Sicily (Enna).[67] But I read the *aition* in relation to the play's discourse of the blurring of Helen with nonhuman entities, which includes Helen's relation with Persephone and with the abducted maidens in general. I argue that Helen Island concludes the patterning of intra-actions and trans-corporeal entanglements of the human and nonhuman in such a way that Helen is ultimately embedded within the play's protean environment. After depicting adverse changes in the conditions of Helen's life (abduction, deception, war), the *aition* of the island serves to symbolize her redemption through a conception of life that sees a fluid network of interconnections between the human, nonhuman, and the wider environment. The island that lies off the coast of Attica is there to remind the audience of this more-than-human ontology of life, in which individuality, indeterminacy, and multiplicity cross over into each other.

Bibliographical References

Alaimo, Stacy. 2010. *Bodily Natures: Science, Environment, and the Material Self*. Bloomington: Indiana University Press.
Alaimo, Stacy. 2020. "New Materialisms." In Sherryl Vint, ed., *After the Human: Culture, Theory and Criticism*, 177–191. Cambridge: Cambridge University Press.
Allan, William. 2008. *Euripides: Helen*. Cambridge: Cambridge University Press.
Anderson, Miranda, Douglas Cairns, and Mark Sprevak, eds. 2018. *Distributed Cognition in Classical Antiquity*. Edinburgh: Edinburgh University Press.
Austin, Norman. 1994. *Helen of Troy and Her Shameless Phantom*. Ithaca: Cornell University Press.
Barad, Karen. 2007. *Meeting the Universe Halfway: Quantum Physics and the Entanglement of Matter and Meaning*. Durham: Duke University Press.
Bassi, Karen. 1987. "Euripides and the Poetics of Deception." Ph.d. diss., Brown University.
Bassi, Karen. 2018. "Morbid Materialism: The Matter of the Corpse in Euripides' *Alcestis*." In Mario Telò and Melissa Mueller, eds., *The Materialities of Greek Tragedy: Objects and Affect in Aeschylus, Sophocles, and Euripides*, 35–48. London: Bloomsbury Academic.
Beacham, Richard. 2007. "Playing Places: The Temporary and the Permanent." In Marianne McDonald and J. Michael Walton, eds., *The Cambridge Companion to Greek and Roman Theatre*, 202–226. Cambridge: Cambridge University Press.
Bennett, Jane. 2010. *Vibrant Matter: A Political Ecology of Things*. Durham: Duke University Press.
Bianchi, Emanuela, Sara Brill, and Brooke Holmes, eds. 2019. *Antiquities beyond Humanism*. Oxford: Oxford University Press.
Blondell, Ruby. 2013. *Helen of Troy: Beauty, Myth, Devastation*. Oxford: Oxford University Press.
Boedeker, Deborah. 2017. "Significant Inconsistencies in Euripides *Helen*." In Laura K. McClure, ed., *A Companion to Euripides*, 243–257. Chichester: Wiley and Sons.
Bradley, Mark, and Shane Butler, eds. 2014–2019. *The Senses in Antiquity*. London: Routledge.
Brown, Bill. 2004. *A Sense of Things: The Object Matter of American Literature*. Chicago: University of Chicago Press.

---

67. For Persephone's rape in Crete, see Bacchylides, fr. 47 from Schol. ad Hesiod, *Theog.* 914; on Sicily, Strabo 6.1.5.

Brown, Bill. 2015. *Other Things*. Chicago: University of Chicago Press.
Burian, Peter. 2007. *Euripides, Helen; With Introduction, Translation and Commentary*. Oxford: Oxford University Press.
Burian, Peter, and Alan Shapiro. 2011. *The Complete Euripides; Volume V: Medea and Other Plays*. Oxford: Oxford University Press.
Cairns, Douglas, and Damien Nelis, eds. 2017. *Emotions in the Classical World: Methods, Approaches, and Directions*. Stuttgart: Franz Steiner Verlag.
Calame, Claude. 1977. *Les chœurs des jeunes filles en Grèce archaïque*. Roma: Edizioni dell'Ateneo e Bizzarri.
Canevaro, Lilah Grace. 2018. *Women of Substance in Homeric Epic: Objects, Gender, Agency*. Oxford: Oxford University Press.
Canevaro, Lilah Grace. 2019. "Materiality and Classics: (Re)Turning to the Material." *JHS* 139: 222–232.
Chaniotis, Angelos. 2012. *Unveiling Emotions: Sources and Methods for the Study of Emotions in the Greek World*. Stuttgart: Franz Steiner Verlag.
Chaniotis, Angelos. 2017. "The Life of Statues: Emotions and Agency." In Douglas Cairns and Damien Nelis, eds., *Emotions in the Classical World: Methods, Approaches, and Directions*, 143–158. Stuttgart: Franz Steiner Verlag.
Chaston, Colleen. 2010. *Tragic Props and Cognitive Function. Aspects of the Function of Images in Thinking*. Leiden: Brill.
Chesi, Giulia Maria, and Francesca Spiegel, eds. 2020. *Classical Literature and Posthumanism*. London: Bloomsbury Academic.
Clarke, M. 2004. "The Semantics of Colour in the Early Greek Word-Hoard." In Liza Cleland, ed., *Colour in the Ancient Mediterranean World*, 131–139. Oxford: Hedges.
Clements, Ashely. 2016. "Colour, Ancient Perception of." *Oxford Classical Dictionary*. https://oxfordre.com/classics/view/10.1093/acrefore/9780199381135.001.0001/acrefore-9780199381135-e-6980. (accessed 15 September 2021)
Clough, Patricia Ticineto, and Jean Halley. 2007. *The Affective Turn: Theorizing the Social*. Durham: Duke University Press.
Day, Joseph W. 2010. *Archaic Greek Epigram and Dedication: Representation and Reperformance*. Cambridge: Cambridge University Press.
Deacy, Susan. 2013. "From Flowery Tales to Heroic Rapes: Virginal Subjectivity in the Mythological Meadow." *Arethusa* 46: 395–413.
Downing, E. 1990. "*Apatê, Agôn*, and Literary Self Reflexivity in Euripides' *Helen*." In Mark Griffith and Donald J. Mastronarde, eds., *Cabinet of the Muses: Essays on Classical and Comparative Literature in Honor of Thomas G. Rosenmeyer*, 1–16. Atlanta: Scholars Press.
Duchemin, Jacqueline. 1940. "L'île d'Hélène dans la tragédie d'Euripide." *REG* 53: 251–253.
Dunn, Francis M. 1996. *Tragedy's End: Closure and Innovation in Euripidean Drama*. Oxford: Oxford University Press.
Foley, Helene P. 2001. *Female Acts in Greek Tragedy*. Princeton: Princeton University Press.
Ford, Andrew Laughlin. 2002. *The Origins of Criticism: Literary Culture and Poetic Theory in Classical Greece*. Princeton: Princeton University Press.
Gaifman, Milette, and Verity Platt. 2018. "Introduction: From Grecian Urn to Embodied Object." *Art History* 41: 402–419.
Goldhill, Simon. 2000. "Civic Ideology and the Problem of Difference: The Politics of Athenian Tragedy, Once Again." *JHS* 120: 34–56.

Goldhill, Simon. 2020. "Conclusions." In Giulia Maria Chesi and Francesca Spiegel, eds., *Classical Literature and Posthumanism*, 331–342. London: Bloomsbury Academic.
Gregg, Melissa, and Gregory J. Seigworth. 2010. *The Affect Theory Reader*. Durham: Duke University Press.
Grethlein, Jonas, and Luuk Huitink. 2017. "Homer's Vividness: An Enactive Approach." *JHS* 137: 67–91.
Grusin, Richard. 2015. *The Nonhuman Turn*. Minneapolis: University of Minnesota Press.
Gumpert, Matthew. 2001. *Grafting Helen: The Abduction of the Classical Past*. Madison: University of Wisconsin Press.
Hall, Edith. 2006. *The Theatrical Cast of Athens: Interactions between Ancient Greek Drama and Society*. Oxford: Oxford University Press.
Halliwell, Stephen. 1993. "The Function and Aesthetics of the Greek Tragic Mask." In Niall W. Slater and Bernhard Zimmermann, eds., *Intertextualität in der Griechisch-Römischen Komödie*, 195–211. Stuttgart: Verlag für Wissenschaft und Forschung.
Haraway, Donna Jeanne. 2003. *The Companion Species Manifesto: Dogs, People, and Significant Otherness*. Chicago: Prickly Paradigm Press.
Harman, Graham. 2002. *Tool-Being: Heidegger and the Metaphysics of Objects*. Chicago: Open Court.
Harman, Graham. 2018. *Object-Oriented Ontology: A New Theory of Everything*. London: Pelican Books.
Henrichs, Albert. 1996. "Why Should I Dance?" Choral Self-Referentiality in Greek Tragedy." *Arion* 3: 56–111.
Hodder, Ian. 2012. *Entangled: An Archaeology of the Relationships between Humans and Things*. Malden, MA: Wiley-Blackwell.
Holmes, Brooke. 2017. "The Body of Western Embodiment: Classical Antiquity and the Early History of a Problem." In Justin E. H. Smith, ed., *Embodiment: A History*, 17–53. Oxford: Oxford University Press.
Irwin, Eleanor. 1974. *Colour Terms in Greek Poetry*. Toronto: Hakkert.
Jansen, Michelle. C. 2012. "Exchange and the *Eidolon*: Analyzing Forgiveness in Euripides' *Helen*." *Comparative Literature Studies* 49: 327–347.
Juffras, Diane M. 1993. "Helen and Other Victims in Euripides' *Helen*." *Hermes* 121: 45–57.
Kannicht, Richard. 1969. *Euripides: Helena*. Heidelberg: Winter.
Kennedy, George A. 1986. "Helen's Web Unraveled," *Arethusa* 19: 5–14.
Kerényi, Karl. 1951. *The Gods of the Greeks*. London: Thames.
Konstan, David. 2006. *The Emotions of Ancient Greeks: Studies in Aristotle and Classical Literature*. Toronto: University of Toronto Press.
Kovacs, David. 2002. *Helen, Phoenician Women, Orestes*. Cambridge: Harvard University Press.
Kraus, Chris, Simon Goldhill, Helene P. Foley, and Jas Elsner, eds. 2007. *Visualizing the Tragic: Drama, Myth, and Ritual in Greek Art and Literature: Essays in Honour of Froma Zeitlin*. Oxford: Oxford University Press.
Latour, Bruno. 2004. "How to Talk about the Body? The Normative Dimension of Science Studies." *Body and Society* 10: 205–229.
Marshall, C. W. 2014. *The Structure and Performance of Euripides' Helen*. Cambridge: Cambridge University Press.
Martin, Richard. P. 2008. "Keens from the Absent Chorus: Troy to Ulster." *Western Folklore* 62: 119–142.

Mastronarde, Donald J. 2002. *Euripides: Medea*. Cambridge: Cambridge University Press.
Meineck, Peter, William Michael Short, and Jennifer Devereaux, eds. 2019. *The Routledge Handbook of Classics and Cognitive Theory*. Abingdon: Routledge.
Mol, Annemarie. 2010. "Actor-Network-Theory: Sensitive Terms and Enduring Tensions." *Kölner Zeitschrift für Soziologie und Sozialpsychologie* 50: 253–269.
Mueller, Melissa. 2010. "Helen's Hands: Weaving for *Kleos* in the *Odyssey*." *Helios* 37: 1–21.
Mueller, Melissa. 2016. *Objects as Actors: Props and the Poetics Performance in Greek Tragedy*. Chicago: University of Chicago Press.
Mureddu, Patrizia. 2003. "Gli stracci di Menelao." *Philologus* 147: 191–204.
Murnaghan, Sheila. 2013. "The Choral Plot of Euripides' *Helen*." In Renaud Gagné and Marianne Govers Hopman, eds., *Choral Mediations in Greek Tragedy*, 155–177. Cambridge: Cambridge University Press.
Padel, Ruth. 1974. "Imagery of the Elsewhere:" Two Choral Odes of Euripides." *CQ* 24: 227–241.
Padgett, J. Michael. 2003. *The Centaur's Smile: The Human Animal in Early Greek Art*. New Haven: Yale University Press.
Porter, James I. 2010. *The Origins of Aesthetic Thought in Ancient Greece: Matter, Sensation, and Experience*. Cambridge: Cambridge University Press.
Porter, James I. 2016. *The Sublime in Antiquity*. Cambridge: Cambridge University Press.
Powers, Melinda. 2014. *Athenian Tragedy in Performance: A Guide to Contemporary Studies and Historical Debates*. Iowa City: University of Iowa Press.
Powers, Sarah. 2010. "Helen's Theatrical *Mêchanê*: Props and Costumes in Euripides' *Helen*." *Theatre Symposium* 18: 23–35.
Pucci, Pietro. 1997. "The *Helen* and Euripides' Comic Art." *ColbyQ* 33: 42–75.
Ragusa, Giuliana, and Patricia A. Rosenmeyer. 2019. "A Delicate Bridegroom: *Habrosunē* in Sappho, Fr. 115V." *CQ* 69: 62–74.
Rehm, Rush. 2002. *The Play of Space: Spatial Transformation in Greek Tragedy*. Princeton: Princeton University Press.
Rekret, Paul. 2016. "A Critique of New Materialisms: Ethics and Ontology." *Subjectivity* 9: 225–245.
Revermann, Martin. 2006. "The Competence of Theatre Audiences in Fifth- and Fourth-Century Athens." *JHS* 126: 99–124.
Roselli, David Kawalko. 2011. *Theater of the People: Spectators and Society in Ancient Athens*. Austin: University of Texas Press.
Rudolph, Kelli. 2016. "Sight and the Presocratics: Approaches to Visual Perception in Early Greek Philosophy." In Michael Squire, ed., *Sight and the Ancient Senses*, 36–53. London: Routledge.
Ryan, Derek. 2013. *Virginia Woolf and the Materiality of Theory: Sex, Animal, Life*. Edinburg: Edinburgh University Press.
Schliephake, Christopher. 2020. "The Environmental Humanities and the Ancient World: Questions and Perspectives." In Louise Westling, Serenella Iovino, and Timo Maran, eds., *Elements in Environmental Humanities*, 1–68. Cambridge: Cambridge University Press.
Scodel, Ruth. 1996. "Δόμων ἄγλαμα: Virgin Sacrifice and Aesthetic Object." *TAPA* 126: 111–128.
Seaman, Myra J. 2007. "Becoming More (than) Human: Affective Posthumanisms, Past and Future." *Journal of Narrative Theory* 37: 246–275.
Sebo, Heather. 2014. "Strife and Starvation: Euripides' *Helen*." *Arethusa* 47: 145–168.
Segal, Charles. 1971. "The Two Worlds of Euripides' *Helen*." *TAPA* 102: 553–614.

Segal, Charles. 1980. *Interpreting Greek Tragedy: Myth, Poetry, Text*. Ithaca: Cornell University Press.
Segal, Charles. 1993. *Euripides and the Poetics of Sorrow: Art, Gender, and Commemoration in Alcestis, Hippolytus, and Hecuba*. Durham: Duke University Press.
Sofer, Andrews. 2016. "Getting on with Things: The Currency of Objects in Theatre and Performance Studies." *Theatre Journal* 68: 673–684.
Sommerstein, Alan H. 2019. *Aeschylus, Suppliants*. Cambridge: Cambridge University Press.
Stanford, William Bedell. 2014. *Greek Tragedy and the Emotions: An Introductory Study*. New York: Routledge.
Steiner, Deborah. 2001. *Images in Mind: Statues in Archaic and Classical Greek Literature and Thought*. Princeton: Princeton University Press.
Steiner, Deborah. 2021. *Choral Constructions in Greek Culture*. Cambridge: Cambridge University Press.
Stieber, Mary. 1999. "A Note on A. *Ag.* 410–28 and E. *Alc.* 347–56." *Mnemosyne* 52: 150–158.
Stieber, Mary. 2011. *Euripides and the Language of Craft*. Leiden: Brill.
Stockdale, Elizabeth. 2020. "The Omen and the Dream: Helen's and Penelope's Visions of the Eagle and the Geese in Homer, *Odyssey* 15.160–178 and 19.535–555." *Helios* 48: 1–15.
Swift, Laura. 2010. *The Hidden Chorus: Echoes of Genre in Tragic Lyric*. Oxford: Oxford University Press.
Swift, Laura. 2016. "Visual Imagery in Parthenaic Song." In Vanessa Cazzato and André Lardinois, eds., *The Look of Lyric: Greek Song and the Visual: Studies in Archaic and Classical Greek Song; Vol. 1*, 255–287. Leiden: Brill.
Taplin, Oliver. 2003. *Greek Tragedy in Action*. New York: Routledge.
Telò, Mario, and Melissa Mueller, eds. 2018. *The Materialities of Greek Tragedy: Objects and Affect in Aeschylus, Sophocles, and Euripides*. London: Bloomsbury Academic.
Thompson, Evan. 2007. "Look Again: Phenomenology and Mental Imagery." *Phenomenology and the Cognitive Sciences* 6: 137–170.
Tsiafakis, Despoina. 2001. "Life and Death at the Hands of a Siren." *Occasional Papers on Antiquities* 10: 7–24.
Vasunia, Phiroze. 2001. *The Gift of the Nile: Hellenizing Egypt from Aeschylus to Alexander*. Berkley: University of California Press.
Vint, Sherryl, ed. 2020. *After the Human: Culture, Theory, and Criticism in the 21st Century*. Cambridge: Cambridge University Press.
Weiberg, Erika. 2020. "The Bed and the Tomb: The Materiality of Signs in Euripides' *Helen*." *Mnemosyne* 73: 729–749.
Weiss, Naomi A. 2018. *Music of Tragedy: Performance and Imagination in Euripidean Theater*. Oakland: University of California Press.
Wiles, David. 2007. *Mask and Performance in Greek Tragedy: From Ancient Festival to Modern Experimentation*. Cambridge: Cambridge University Press.
Willink, C.W. 1990. "The *Parodos* of Euripides' *Helen* (164–90)." *CQ* 40: 77–99.
Worman, Nancy. 1997. "The Body as Argument: Helen in Four Greek Texts." *CA* 16: 151–203.
Worman, Nancy. 1999. "The Ties that Bind: Transformations of Costume and Connection in Euripides' *Heracles*." *Ramus* 28: 89–107.
Worman, Nancy. 2015. "Exquisite Corpses and Other Bodies in the Electra Plays." *BICS* 58: 77–92.
Worman, Nancy. 2020. *Tragic Bodies: Edges of the Human in Greek Drama*. London: Bloomsbury Academic.

Wright, Matthew. 2005. *Euripides' Escape Tragedies*. Oxford: Oxford University Press.
Zeitlin, Froma. 1981. "Travesties of Gender and Genre in Aristophanes' *Thesmophoriazouse*." *Critical Inquiry* 8: 301–327.
Zeitlin, Froma. 1994. "The Artful Eye: Vision, Ecphrasis and Spectacle in Euripidean Theatre." In Simon Goldhill and Robin Osborne, eds., *Art and Text in Ancient Greek Culture*, 138–196. Cambridge: Cambridge University Press.
Zeitlin, Froma. 1996. *Playing the Other: Gender and Society in Classical Greek Literature*. Chicago: University of Chicago Press.
Zeitlin, Froma. 2010. "The Lady Vanishes: Helen and Her Phantom in Euripidean Drama." In Phillip Mitsis and Christos Tsagalis, eds., *Allusion, Authority, and Truth: Critical Perspectives on Greek Poetic and Rhetorical Praxis*, 263–282. Berlin and New York: De Gruyter.
Zuckerberg, Donna. 2016. "The Clothes Make the Man: Aristophanes and the Ragged Hero in Euripides' *Helen*." *CP* 111: 203–223.
Zweig, Bella. 1999. "Euripides' *Helen* and Female Rites of Passage." In Mark W. Padilla, ed., *Rites of Passage in Ancient Greece: Literature, Religion, Society*, 158–180. Lewisburg: Bucknell University Press.

Language and Agency in Sappho's Brothers Poem

ALEXANDRA LEEWON SCHULTZ

Notes on Provenance

The papyrus fragment containing the text of the Brothers Poem (P.Sapph.Obbink) has no established provenance, since Dirk Obbink's accounts of provenance have been exposed as fabrications. There is further reason to believe the fragment was looted and sold illegally on the antiquities black market: P.Sapph.Obbink comes from the same book roll as the illegally-acquired Hobby Lobby/Green Collection fragments that were returned to Egypt in January 2021. The present whereabouts of P.Sapph.Obbink are unknown. This article engages with the text of the poem and its scholarly reception, but it is equally important that we continue to investigate the object's history. I draw the reader's attention to the important work by Roberta Mazza and others.[1]

Introduction: Approaching Sappho through Alcaeus

What role should gender play in interpreting Sappho's poetry? Did Sappho reproduce ancient gender norms, which typically defined woman as the negative antithesis of man (man/woman, public/private, active/passive, powerful/powerless)? Or can Sappho's poetry offer alternative conceptions of gender roles and agency? These are genuine questions, as we lack contextual data to explain how Sappho composed poetry in a male-dominated society where speech was power. What did it mean for a woman to compose songs in archaic Greece?

From considerations of style to reconstructions of performance context, Sappho's gender has led many critics to approach her poetry differently from that of other lyric poets.[2] Historically this double standard has been most obvious in discussions of her erotic poetry. Yet a double standard has also impacted scholarship on the

---

1. See recently Nongbri 2019, Sampson and Uhlig 2019, Higgins 2020, Mazza 2020, Sabar 2020, Sampson 2020. I am grateful to colleagues who advised me on the ethics of publishing on unprovenanced antiquities. I decided to publish this article, knowing that it may further increase the value of a looted object, because I felt that it was important to add a feminist critique to the scholarly debate on the poem.
2. Discussed in Lefkowitz 1973, Hallett 1979, Winkler 1981, DeJean 1989, Parker 1993.

recently discovered Brothers Poem; although many of its features can be found in the work of other lyric poets, scholars have interpreted them in gendered terms. Take the poem's form. Joel Lidov, who perceptively observes that the poem's "prosaic" syntax, style, and meter are more typical of Alcaeus than Sappho, concludes that Sappho employs these devices to craft an "awkward" persona (2016, 101–105). Or its content: male poets also pray to Hera, but scholars interpret Sappho's prayer to the goddess as an admission of powerlessness, since women "cannot do anything more active than talk or pray" (Swift 2018, 84).[3]

In general, scholars are preoccupied with the poem's gender norms and power dynamics. Regarding the interlocutor's identity, some argue that a man would not "babble" (θρύλησθα) or take orders from the speaker (σὲ δ' οὐ χρῆ [...]), while others doubt that a woman would have the "authority" to command the speaker to pray (πέμπην ἔμε καὶ κέλεσθαι [...]).[4] Meanwhile, though some critics view the speaker as "a person of authority,"[5] most have concluded that the poem depicts women's lack of agency.[6] It is worth noting that nothing in the poem's text genders the speaking 'I' as a woman. Perhaps the initial stanza originally included a gender marker, and certainly the performance would have gendered the speaking voice. However, it may be the case that Sappho and her audience were simply less interested in issues of gender than we are.[7] The poem's gender dynamics still merit scholarly attention, but interpretations that isolate Sappho from a wider lyric tradition risk missing what is unique about her poetry—and often import modern prejudice without methodological justification.

In this article, I reevaluate the style and internal dynamics of the Brothers Poem by reading it alongside Alcaeus's poetry and argue that Sappho depicts women endowed with agency. Critics have thus far mainly focused on reconstructing the religious context that Sappho and Alcaeus shared,[8] but by comparing their language we can illuminate how to read Sappho's poetry both as archaic lyric and as female. In Part I of this article, building on previous studies of poetic diction,

---

3. See also Bierl 2016, 326, 329–333; Gribble 2016, 59–63; Kurke 2016, 241–242; Mueller 2016, 32; Stehle 2016, 290.

4. The interlocutor's identity is discussed in Bettenworth 2014; Nünlist 2014; Obbink 2014b, 41–42; West 2014, 8–9; Neri 2015, 58–62; Bierl 2016, 327–334; Kurke 2016, 239–249; Lardinois 2016, 182–184; Stehle 2016; Swift 2018, 83–84.

5. Lidov 2016, 104; see also Mueller 2016, 34: "She takes charge of the situation."

6. E.g., Bierl 2016, 333: "a prudent and submissive woman"; Stehle 2016, 291: "She remains a woman dependent on the male members of her family"; Swift 2018, 83–85: "powerless," "cannot take an active role."

7. I thank the anonymous reader who brought this issue to my attention.

8. On the shared religious context see Henrichs 2014, Pirenne-Delforge and Pironti 2014, Nagy 2015 and 2016 (with Nagy 2007), and Boedeker 2016. Kurke (2016, 242 note 17) provides additional bibliography.

imagery, and themes common to the Lesbian poets, I address features that the Brothers Poem shares with the poetry of Alcaeus.[9] Some of these elements in the Brothers Poem have been read as gendered or as admissions of powerlessness, but I argue that these features should be understood instead as a 'poetics of misfortune'.[10] In Section II, I demonstrate that the Brothers Poem must be read not only against the backdrop of Sappho's other 'brother poems,' but also alongside her erotic poetry. Drawing on feminist scholarship that highlights the woman-centeredness and double consciousness of her erotic poems, I argue that Sappho used similar stylistic features in the Brothers Poem to adapt a traditional repertoire of poetry and myth in a way that privileged the experiences of women.[11]

While audience and performance context are not the central focus of this paper, my reading has implications for the way we envision Sappho performing her music. Some scholars have posited that the Brothers Poem was monodic poetry performed at gatherings of aristocratic women;[12] others, that the Brothers Poem was choral poetry performed at a religious festival for Hera.[13] This disagreement stems from the now-familiar debate over whether Sappho primarily performed among adult, aristocratic women from politically-allied families who formed an association akin to Alcaeus's *hetaireia*,[14] or whether she educated choruses of pubescent girls (*parthenoi*) about sex and love in order to prepare them for marriage.[15]

---

9. In particular Lidov 2016. On Sappho's engagement with traditionally masculine poetic discourse and aristocratic values, see Kurke 1992; Parker 1993; Williamson 1995, 84–89, 136–140; Wilson 1996, 1–20, 172–185; Aloni 1997, passim; Stehle 1997, 262–318; Parker 2005; Greene 2008.

10. Though the speaker does not specify the source of her misfortune, many have speculated that it relates to the political turmoil of archaic Mytilene; see, e.g., Liberman 2014, 11; Bierl 2016, 326; Gribble 2016, 46, 52; Kurke 2016, 238, 241, 251, 254; Lardinois 2016, 176–177; Lidov 2016, 83–84; Raaflaub 2016, 139–140; Stehle 2016, 276–277, 284.

11. Winkler 1981 and Skinner 1993; also Stehle 1981 and 1990, Snyder 1997, Greene 2008.

12. Stehle 2016, 271–272; see also Caciagli 2016, 437–441. Obbink (2015, 9) suggests a convivial, if not sympotic, performance setting. Gribble (2016, 64–67) envisions a female audience, but also argues that the song was intended as personal advice for Charaxos and Larichos.

13. Nagy 2015 and 2016; Bierl 2016, 336; Lidov 2016, 84–87, 104, 107–108; Mueller 2016, 35. The speaker's reference to a future ritual occasion does not mean that the Brothers Poem was actually performed at a festival to Hera: Lardinois 2016, 184–85, and D'Alessio 2018.

14. As argued in Parker 1993 and Stehle 1997, 262–288; see also Page 1955, 126–140; Trumpf 1973, 160; Most 1982, 95–96; Burnett 1983, 209; Gentili 1988, 81; Caciagli 2011, 41–91. Stehle (1997, 276–277) views Sappho's songs about her brothers, invectives against other women, and fragments that allude to politics as best suited to a sympotic setting. Skinner (2014, 73–74) discusses new visual evidence for female symposia.

15. See esp. Merkelbach 1957, Calame 1977, Hallett 1979, Burnett 1983, Gentili 1988, Lardinois 1994; more recently, Tsomis 2001, 22–37; Ferrari 2010, passim; Lardinois 2010; Benelli 2017, passim. Caciagli (2011) envisions multiple performance settings, but similarly argues that Sappho formed pederastic relationships with adolescents to prepare them for marriage. Cantarella (1992,

It is not my purpose to revisit this controversy. More recent studies of pragmatics, reperformance, and the reception of lyric poetry have critiqued such attempts to extract an original, historical performance setting from poetic speech,[16] and my analysis of the Brothers Poem does not depend on a particular view of its performance context. Nevertheless, the similarities I note between Sappho's and Alcaeus's poetry should encourage us to reconsider the issue. To my mind these similarities suggest that Sappho performed some of her music at a setting akin to the symposium and that at social gatherings within families and aristocratic alliances, women and men forged a common poetic tradition.[17] Most importantly, these similarities urge us to view Sappho not as a schoolmistress, chorus leader, priestess of Aphrodite, "sensual consciousness raiser," or prostitute,[18] but as a poet among lyric poets.

I Sappho, Alcaeus, and the Poetics of Misfortune

Although many scholars have recognized that the Brothers Poem shares its historical, religious, and perhaps performance context with Alcaeus's poetry, few have entertained the possibility of a shared literary tradition.[19] The exception is Joel Lidov, whose 2016 study of structure and style in the Brothers Poem and select fragments of Alcaeus forms our starting point. Lidov perceptively notes that the Brothers Poem, Alcaeus fr. 129, and several other fragments often identified as prayers do not fit the standard prayer model: invocation, argument, request. Instead, they seem to form a corpus of songs about safe returns from danger, with the underlying structure of first emphasizing the present danger, then requesting immediate assistance, and finally imagining a brighter future.[20] Beyond his important observations on the thematic and structural parallels between these poems, Lidov also scrutinizes the diction of the Brothers Poem. Compared to the rest of Sappho's

---

83–84), Parker (1993), Skinner (1993 and 2014, 84–91), Greene (1994, 54–55), and Konstan (1997, 47–48) critique the view that female homoeroticism functioned like male pederasty and socialized girls for marriage.

16. E.g., Yatromanolakis 2007 and 2009, 216–220; D'Alessio 2009; Hunter and Uhlig 2017; Budelmann and Phillips 2018a; and esp. D'Alessio 2018.

17. Vidan's study (2003, esp. 12–31) of Bosnian oral poetry performed by women offers intriguing parallels. See Nagy 2007 on festive settings where Alcaeus and Sappho could have met.

18. Quoted from Hallett 1979, 460. Schlesier (2013) argues that Sappho was a *hetaira*.

19. Historical context: see note 10 above, with Page 1955, 130–133, 149–243, 223–226; Burnett 1983, 107–120; and Gagné 2013, 210–226 on the political history of archaic Mytilene in Sappho's and Alcaeus's lifetimes. For the religious context, see note 8 above; for the performance context, note 12. O'Connell (2018) discusses fascinating parallels between the Brothers Poem and "songs of welcome" by other lyric poets, esp. Archilochus fr. 24.

20. Lidov 2016, 59–63. See also Mueller 2016, 35–36, 40–43, and Gribble 2016, 59–64.

corpus, the poem's handling of word-end within the Sapphic stanza is unusually monotonous (whereas Alcaeus tends to be more regular). Moreover, the poem contains an abnormally high number of subjunctives; it employs the only hortatory subjunctive and sole use of χρή in all of Sappho's poetry (both found regularly in Alcaeus); and its syntax is convoluted, even prosaic.[21] Lidov interprets these features as intentional slips designed to make the persona seem "awkward," the marks of a poet skilled at personifying different speaking voices, rather than the failings of an awkward poem as some have supposed.[22]

Lidov's careful study contributes greatly to our understanding of the Brothers Poem's structure and diction. However, his observation that many stylistic features of the Brothers Poem are found regularly in Alcaeus's corpus (the hortatory subjunctive, χρή, and the conditional relative with κε[23]) argues against interpreting them as intentionally awkward. Rather, these similarities suggest that the Brothers Poem draws on a shared stylistic repertoire. In fact, the correspondences between the Brothers Poem and Alcaeus's poetry run deeper than the structural and syntactic similarities Lidov has observed.

To explore these similarities, I begin with Alcaeus fr. 129:[24]

] . ρα . α τόδε Λέσβιοι
. . .] . . . . εὔδειλον τέμενος μέγα
ξῦνον κά[τε]σσαν, ἐν δὲ βώμοις
    ἀθανάτων μακάρων ἔθηκαν
κἀπωνύμασσαν ἀντίαον Δία   5
σὲ δ' Αἰολήιαν [κ]υδαλίμαν θέον
πάντων γενέθλαν, τὸν δὲ τέρτον
    τόνδε κεμήλιον ὠνύμασσ[α]ν
Ζόννυσον ὠμήσταν. ἄ[γι]τ' εὔνοον
θῦμον σκέθοντες ἀμμετέρα[ς] ἄρας   10
ἀκούσατ', ἐκ δὲ τῶν[δ]ε μόχθων
    ἀργαλέας τε φύγας ῥ[ύεσθε.

---

21. Specifically the string of infinitives in the first three stanzas and the conditional relative clause starting with τῶν in the fourth stanza (Lidov 2016, 101–106).

22. Lidov 2016, 104–109. For examples of the poem's negative reception see West's comments quoted in Obbink 2014a and 2015, 4; Liberman 2014, 8; Mueller 2016, 27; Stehle 2016, 268. One wonders whether their criticisms of the poem as hastily composed, illogical, disappointing, "frigid juvenilia" (a personal favorite) would be phrased differently were the author not Sappho.

23. Found in Alcaeus fr. 358.6–7 (Lidov 2016, 103 note 75) and possibly fr. 70.8–9 (Obbink 2014b, 44).

24. All numbering and quotations of Sappho and Alcaeus are taken from Voigt 1971 unless otherwise specified. All translations are my own.

τὸν Ὕρραον δὲ πα[ῖδ]α πεδελθέτω
κήνων Ἐ[ρίννυ]ς ὥς ποτ' ἀπώμνυμεν
τόμοντες ἄ .. [´ .]v . v   15
    μηδάμα μηδ' ἔνα τὼν ἐταίρων
ἀλλ' ἢ θάνοντες γᾶν ἐπιέμμενοι
κείσεσθ' ὑπ' ἄνδρων οἲ τότ' ἐπικ ΄ . ην
ἤπειτα κακκτάνοντες αὔτοις
    δᾶμον ὐπὲξ ἀχέων ῤύεσθαι.   20
κήνων ὀ φύσκων οὐ διελέξατο
πρὸς θῦμον, ἀλλὰ βραϊδίως πόσιν
ἔ]μβαις ἐπ' ὀρκίοισι δάπτει
    τὰν πόλιν ἄμμι δέδ[.] .. [.] . ί . αις
οὐ κὰν νόμον [.]ον .. [   ] ΄ [ ]   25

here the inhabitants of Lesbos
    ... founded a great sunny precinct
to be held in common, and in it they built
    altars for the immortal gods
and they called upon Zeus of Suppliants
and you, glorious Aeolian goddess,
mother of all, and third
    they called this god Kemelios,
Dionysus the Raw-Eater. Come,
listen to our prayers with
kindheartedness, and save us from
    this suffering and painful exile.
As for the son of Hyrrhas, let a Fury
pursue him for those things, since once
we swore sacrificing ...
    never any companion
but either to lie dead, cloaked in earth,
at the hands of the men who at that time...
or else to kill them and
    save the people from misery.
The Fatso didn't take that
to heart, but trampled over his oaths
without a second thought and now
    he gobbles down the city while we...
unlawfully...

Fr. 129 can be divided roughly in half. In the first half (1–12), the speaker sets the scene at the precinct to the Lesbian triad (Zeus, Hera, and Dionysus) and calls on the gods for assistance.[25] He asks that the gods listen to "our prayers" and grant protection from toils and exile. In the second half (13–25), he pivots to additional hopes that a Fury take vengeance on Pittacus, who was formerly allied with Alcaeus and his companions. They once swore an oath to die fighting their enemies or to kill their enemies and save the city. But Pittacus trampled on their oaths and is now consuming the city to the detriment of "us." At this point the fragment becomes too tattered to read much more, but Alcaeus may have mentioned Myrsilus (μύρσιλ[ο, 28), the tyrant whom Alcaeus and Pittacus once opposed together, but for whom Pittacus abandoned Alcaeus and his companions.

Fr. 129 forms a locus classicus for pragmatic interpretations of Alcaeus as a symposiast addressing his *hetaireia*, an approach pioneered by Wolfgang Rösler and widely adopted thereafter.[26] According to a functionalist reading of sympotic poetry, its key purpose was to foster solidarity among audience members, often achieved by contrasting the sympotic group (characterized by community, loyalty, and pleasurable consumption) to an Other that represents the dangers of isolation and faithlessness.[27] Fr. 129 employs an extreme version of the factionalist poetics that runs through much of Alcaeus's stasiotic poetry. Yet, even without turning to such extratextual realities, we can observe how the speaker frames the misfortune he and his companions face.

First, Alcaeus divides the figures of the song into two diametrically opposed groups: 'us' versus 'them.'[28] He and his companions form the song's first-person plural, and he speaks for them throughout: there is no 'I,' only 'we.'[29] He calls on the gods to listen to "our prayers" (ἀμμετέρας ἄρας, 10), recalls a time when "we swore an oath" (ἀπώμνυμεν, 14), and condemns Pittacus for devouring the city and hurting "us" (ἄμμι, 24) in some way. Pittacus was once one of 'us,' part of the in-group, the circle of honorable men who swore oaths of loyalty. But now Pittacus has joined 'them,' the men they swore to be killed by or to kill (18–19). The poem

---

25. I view the speakers of Alcaeus's and Sappho's poetry as poetic personae and will sometimes refer to 'Alcaeus' and 'Sappho' in quotes when distinguishing the poetic persona from the poet, but I recognize that poet and persona cannot be artificially separated; see Stehle 2016, 267–268, on this point.
26. Rösler 1980, with 191–204 on fr. 129.
27. Rösler 1980, 33–41; Donlan 1985; Stehle 1997, 216–217, 223–227; Elmer 2013, 157, 161.
28. See also Romney 2019, who has independently reached an analysis of Alcaeus fr. 129 similar to my own.
29. See also frr. 6 and 70, as well as 335, where advice addressed to an individual is framed as the collective activity of an 'us'-group in response to misfortune. Rösler (1980, 38) lists occurrences of "we" and "our" in Alcaeus's poetry.

draws a line down the middle with the speaker, his companions, the gods, the city, and the law on one side; and Pittacus and possibly Myrsilus on the other side, pursued by an avenging Fury. It is a Manichaean world of black and white, either/or, right or wrong, kill or be killed, with us or against us.

Besides delineating 'us' versus 'them,' Alcaeus also characterizes these two sides in opposing terms. He villainizes Pittacus rather straightforwardly. For breaking his oath, Pittacus—no longer "the son of Hyrrhas" but now a gluttonous "Fatso" devouring the city—should be punished by a Fury.[30] Furthermore, Alcaeus casts Pittacus as a tyrannical figure, isolated and autocratic in opposition to the group's collectivity and camaraderie. Not only is Pittacus categorically excluded from his former companions, but he has become the opposite of the ideal male aristocratic *hetairos* who abides by oaths, demonstrates courage in battle, is willing to die for a shared cause, and above all else is defined by loyalty to his friends.

More subtle are the ways in which Alcaeus exculpates and valorizes his companions despite their apparent failure. In the extant portion of the song Alcaeus blames Pittacus for their misery and invests hope for the future in the gods. This rhetorical sleight of hand exculpates them from all blame and responsibility by representing past failures and future endeavors as out of their hands. At the same time, Alcaeus subtly valorizes his downtrodden companions by conjuring images of collective activity.[31] At the opening he sings of the Lesbians "collectively" (ξῦνον, 3) founding a holy precinct. Furthermore, the precinct belongs jointly to the gods Zeus, Hera ("the mother of all"), and Dionysus. These harmonious communities of men and of gods and the pious, cooperative venture that brought them all together stand in stark contrast to Pittacus's treachery, while also serving as praise for Alcaeus's companions' past loyalty and a model for the future.[32] Furthermore, Alcaeus reminds them of the oaths that, much like collective song-making, were speech-acts that bound the group together. Thus, even in their defeat they retain their dignity.

Alcaeus further valorizes his companions by drawing a subtle parallel to the gods through repetition and metrical response: at lines 11–12 he asks the gods to

---

30. Kurke (1994, 84) argues that Alcaeus honors Pittacus with a patronymic when describing his former friend as part of the *hetaireia*, although Gagné (2013, 216–217) counters that 'Hyrrhas' and 'Hyrradios' may in fact be derogatory terms insulting Pittacus's low birth, rather than the name of his father. See also Hipponax fr. 115W, which imagines a vicious fate for a former *hetairos* who betrayed his friends, with Stehle 1997, 225–226, on how expelling the traitor from the group "unites singer and audience in aggression directed outward."

31. Cf. Stehle 1997, 233, on the Lesbian women celebrating religious rites as an "alluring image of collective purpose that has escaped the *hetaireia*" in Alcaeus fr. 130.

32. Kurke (1994, 87–88) argues that Alcaeus represents the Lesbians as a perfect, unified community to forge consensus among his *hetaireia*, while Boterf (2018, 388–391) maintains that Alcaeus contrasts the Lesbians' successful foundation to the failure of Alcaeus's companions after Pittacus's betrayal.

"rescue (us) from these toils and painful exile" (ἐκ δὲ τῶνδε μόχθων / ἀργαλέας τε φύγας ῥ[ύεσθε]). Two stanzas later he recalls his companions' oath to "rescue the people from distress" (δᾶμον ὐπὲξ ἀχέων ῥύεσθαι, 20). If the supplement ῥ[ύεσθε] at line 12 is correct, Alcaeus twice construes a form of ῥύεσθαι at the end of a strophe, with the preposition (ὐπ)έκ and the genitive, to describe someone powerful saving someone in distress.[33] In so doing he implicitly equates the relationship of the all-powerful gods to man with the relationship of his companions to the *damos*: both they and the gods are powerful bulwarks against malicious elements. In light of how Alcaeus portrays agency in the poem, the comparison between the gods and his companions is a particularly clever rhetorical move. In reality they may be losers unable to save the city or even themselves, but when Alcaeus recalls their oath they can become godlike saviors again, if only in song. Thus, by demarcating 'us' versus 'them,' privileging collective action over isolation, villainizing Pittacus, and valorizing his friends, Alcaeus reframes misfortune as an opportunity to band together.

These same rhetorical strategies surface in Sappho's poetry, especially in songs that describe personal enmities or reference political conflict. In her most vicious songs, she attacks women from rival families or women who, much like Pittacus, betrayed Sappho and her friends for the enemy.[34] For example, in fr. 71 addressed to Mica, Sappho reviles her former companion for choosing the "friendship of the women of the Penthelid house," which she contrasts with something of "ours" (possibly "our company").[35] Sappho reminds her companions of their beautiful song-making and demonizes Mica as a backstabber, who has cut herself off from the sweet singing of their privileged circle.[36] As in Alcaeus fr. 129, Sappho delineates 'us' versus 'them,' insults the woman who betrayed her companions, and reminds her audience of the speech-act that bound and continues to bind them together. Fr. 71 represents Mica's betrayal as her loss rather than theirs.

Other songs use these same rhetorical strategies to explore the ramifications of misfortune without focusing on a hated enemy; instead, they emphasize what the

---

33. Kurke (1994, 88) also notes that both occur immediately before mentions of Pittacus, and interprets this repetition as linking the exiles' salvation to that of the *damos*.

34. Williamson 1995, 87–88, and Parker 2005, 6–9, 16.

35. Sappho fr. 71.3–4:]γ φιλότ[ατ'] ἤλεο Πενθιλήαγ[/]δα κα[κό]τροπ', ἄμμα[. Mica may also have been Sappho's lover (Gentili 1988, 261 note 42), though this is not clear from the fragment.

36. See also fr. 55 attacking a woman who will be forgotten when she dies, since she has "no share in the roses of Pieria" (οὐ γὰρ **πεδέχηις βρόδων** / τὼν ἐν Πιερίας, 2–3); instead, in a grim reversal, she will flit invisibly "among the dim shades" of the underworld (**πεδ'** ἀμαύρων νεκύων, 4). Ferrari (2010, 19–23) discusses five fragments of P.Oxy. 1787 which seem to form a poem mentioning exile, Artemis taking vengeance on Andromeda, and beautiful music.

speaker has lost and the emotional repercussions. For example, in fr. 5, newly supplemented by papyri that were acquired illegally by the Green Collection and recently repatriated to Egypt, 'Sappho' voices concern about a brother whose misconduct has jeopardized his family's social standing.[37] In the first part of the song she prays to the Nereids that her brother return home safely, atone for his mistakes, bring joy to his friends, and bring misery to his enemies (5.1–7). At this point the prayer to the Nereids ends and the speaker transitions to a series of wishes that more directly concern herself and her family. She hopes that "we never have any (enemy)" (γένοιτο δ' ἄμμι / **μηδάμα μηδ' εἶς**, 5.7–8) in language similar to Alcaeus's oath "never [to betray?] any one of our companions" (**μηδάμα μηδ' ἕνα** τὼν ἑταίρων, 129.16). 'Sappho' then wishes that her brother bring *her* more honor, since previously his actions incurred the "blame of the citizens," but now he has seen the error of his ways (5.9–16).

As in Alcaeus fr. 129, the speaker of Sappho fr. 5 refers to suffering that has resulted from loss of public standing, prays to the gods to intervene, and distinguishes 'us' from the enemy.[38] And although the speaker of fr. 5 wishes her absent brother well (unlike Alcaeus's wish for Pittacus to be punished), both speakers externalize blame by attributing present misfortune to a third party's failings. Finally, in both songs, these concerns loop back to the chief party of interest: 'us,' whose difficulties the speaker articulates. Despite differences in tone and the parties concerned, the two songs confront the loss of social standing through similar phrases, structures, and rhetorical techniques in such a way as to unite the first-person plural in its misfortune and to provide hope for a reversal of fortune.

In sum, Alcaeus and Sappho deploy a similar set of strategies for addressing misfortune. As we have seen, in addition to similar phrasing, their shared strategies included defining an in-group ('us') against an out-group ('them'), praising collective action and mutual responsibility, valorizing one's companions, pinning blame on a third party, and enlisting the help of the gods. In Alcaeus's poetry, many of these rhetorical techniques have been interpreted within the framework of the symposium, where a singer aimed to solidify loyalties among his companions and dignify their suffering. Whether or not one believes that Sappho also performed at gatherings among fellow aristocrats, she did employ similar techniques to describe hardship in her own poetry, especially in poems that reference social standing and political conflict. The Lesbian poets inherited their craft from a tradition of singers

---

37. Perhaps a political error as Williamson (1995, 138–139) has argued (see also Aloni 1997, lxxi), but not an affair with a courtesan (Lidov 2002). Stehle (1997, 283) argues that Sappho performed fr. 5 before women from politically allied families affected by her brother's misconduct. Williamson (1995, 86, 137–138) and Caciagli (2016, 442–443) discuss male discourse around social values and politics in fr. 5. Obbink (2016a) provides the new text.

38. Along with the structural parallels that Lidov (2016, 61–65, 68) describes.

who had developed vocabulary, themes, meters, and melodies for singing about the vast range of human experience, including loss. I term these techniques a *poetics of misfortune* from which both Sappho and Alcaeus drew.

I now turn to the Brothers Poem, whose speaker communicates above all else her present misfortune. She is anxious about Charaxos's return, considers the poem's first-person plural ('us') to be in peril, reflects on changes of fortune and the fact that Zeus can enrich whomever he chooses, and anticipates that 'we' will be freed from anguish if Larichos grows up one day. Although she does not specify the source of her troubles, it seems that she is in considerable danger without an adult male family member at home and she hopes to regain her former social standing. As we will see below, the language and rhetorical poses Sappho employs to frame this loss draw on the poetics of misfortune.

Like Alcaeus fr. 129 and Sappho fr. 5 above, the Brothers Poem can be divided roughly in two. The first half of the poem frames the dramatic setting and includes an (indirect) prayer to the gods. The poem becomes intelligible at line 5, where 'Sappho' accuses her interlocutor of prattling on about Charaxos and urges a better course of action (5–13):[39]

ἀλλ' ἄϊ θρύλησθα Χάραξον ἔλθην   5
νᾶϊ σὺν πλήαι. τὰ μέν, οἴομαι, Ζεῦς
οἶδε σύμπαντές τε θέοι· σὲ δ'οὐ χρῆ
    ταῦτα νόησθαι,
ἀλλὰ καὶ πέμπην ἔμε καὶ κέλεσθαι
πόλλα λίσσεσθαι βασίληαν Ἥραν   10
ἐξίκεσθαι τυίδε σάαν ἄγοντα
    νᾶα Χάραξον
κἄμμ' ἐπεύρην ἀρτέμεας.

... but you always babble about Charaxos coming
with a full ship. These matters, I suppose, Zeus
knows about, and *all* the gods; but you shouldn't
    think about that,
rather you should send me and bid me
to beseech queen Hera with many prayers
that Charaxos arrive here steering a
    sound ship
and find us unscathed.

---

39. All quotations of the Brothers Poem are taken from Obbink 2016a; see Benelli 2017, 97–98, on retaining the papyrus's πλέαι. All translations are my own.

Instead of babbling uselessly about Charaxos and his lucrative voyage, the speaker advocates taking matters into one's own hands. Only the gods know what will happen—that knowledge is outside the purview of mortals. But in the meantime, she should be sent to pray to Hera for Charaxos's *safe* return, and moreover that upon his return he find 'us' unscathed.

Alcaeus's poetry can illuminate Sappho's diction. As noted earlier, this passage contains the only use in all of Sappho's corpus of χρή, a word regularly used by Alcaeus.[40] It is not clear why a word happily encountered in Alcaeus's poetry would be interpreted as "prosaic" or intentionally "awkward" in Sappho's voice.[41] It is equally plausible that Sappho's rebuke parallels the sorts of instructions and admonitions that Alcaeus sang before his companions. In fr. 249, for example, Alcaeus contrasts proper behavior on land to conduct at sea: "From land it is necessary [χρῆ] to plan ahead for sailing [...] but whenever someone is at sea, necessity [ἀνάγκα] runs (?) to the present."[42] Likewise, in fr. 335, Alcaeus tells Bycchis that "There is no need [οὐ χρῆ] to surrender one's heart to troubles," and that instead he should drown his sorrows in wine. Sappho gives more practical advice: there is "no need [οὐ χρῆ]" to chatter on uselessly about something only the gods can predict—instead, pray to Queen Hera.[43]

Alcaeus's poetry can illuminate another aspect of the Brothers Poem, namely, the prospective prayer to Hera. Many critics have interpreted the prayer in gendered terms as the product of the speaker's status as a woman and concomitant lack of agency.[44] According to this view, 'Sappho' and her interlocutor "cannot do

---

40. Alcaeus frr. 249.6, 332.1, 335.1, 368.2. See also ἀνάγκα (ἐστιν) in frr. 75.6, 249.9. I accent χρῆ with a circumflex when quoting Sappho and Alcaeus, but otherwise χρή with an acute.

41. *Pace* Lidov 2016, 102–106.

42. Alcaeus fr. 249.6-9: ἐ]κ γᾶς χρῆ προΐδην πλό[ον / αἴ τις δύναται κα]ὶ π[αλ]άμαν ἔ[χ]η, / ἐπεὶ δέ κ' ἐν π]όγ[τωι γ]ένηται / τῶι παρέοντι †τρέχειν† ἀνά]γκα. See also Uhlig 2018, 86–87.

43. Alcaeus frequently refers to Zeus as "King" (Κρονίδαις βασίλευς, frr. 38a.9, 296a.3, 387; Κρονίδαι [...] παμβασίληϊ, fr. 308b.3-4), a title that reflects a view of the world as a patriarchy dominated by a legitimate ruler (Burnett 1983, 119). I suggest tentatively that, in calling Hera "Queen," Sappho recognizes Hera's own supreme authority (cf. Nagy 2016, 458–459, 477), rather than deriving the title straightforwardly from her status as Zeus's wife (*pace* Henrichs 2014, 7, and Bierl 2016, 314; cf. Stehle 1997, 299 on Aphrodite's role in fr. 1). Boedeker (2016, 205–206) and Kurke (2016, 244, 249) offer different interpretations of these titles.

44. Thus Bierl 2016, 332: "Archaic Greek women have a subordinate role in society but can exert influence in their cultic and religious roles." Gribble 2016, 60: "Prayer is an act appropriate to, and beneficial for, a woman in these circumstances." Kurke 2016, 241–242: "Sappho here talks about the doings of men out in the public world [...] but all of this is filtered through the intimate domestic sphere of the family and women's proper religious activity of prayer." Mueller 2016, 32: "Sappho and her mother remain ensconced in their private domestic space; their only contact with the broader public is through prayer." Stehle 2016, 290: "Prayer is one form of discourse that was

anything more active than talk or pray," as if prayer were merely a feminine proxy for the real actions taken by men. Within such a restrictive view of gender roles (closer perhaps to fifth-century Athens than archaic Ionia), the Brothers Poem acknowledges women's powerlessness to effect change. Meanwhile, the poem's internal prayer supposedly mirrors the poem's historical performance at a religious festival to Hera, thus confining women's speech and agency to religious occasions both within and without the poem.

It is strange to encounter in discussions of Sappho's poetry so great an emphasis on women's lack of agency. I am not denying that religious activity was a socially sanctioned means for women to speak and act in public, and there are productive discussions to be had around the literary trope of women praying for absent men.[45] But religious rituals should not be viewed as alternatives to real action, nor as activity limited to women. A gendered interpretation would need to address how Sappho's prayer differs from, for example, the prayers to Hera composed by Alcman and Alcaeus, and would furthermore need to argue that such differences derive from Sappho's status as a woman rather than choices she made as a poet.[46]

A comparison with Alcaeus reveals significant similarities and differences in poetic technique. In fr. 129, Alcaeus prays to the gods for relief from the suffering and exile Pittacus has inflicted on his companions. Although the only concrete action he takes in the song is to pray, I imagine that few critics would interpret his prayer as gendered behavior. In the Brothers Poem the speaker's prayer also functions as a means of taking action to combat suffering. That is why she tells her interlocutor not to give in to futile lines of thinking and insists on being dispatched to pray to Hera. Furthermore, the key difference such a comparison illuminates is not that the Brothers Poem's female speaker conforms to ancient gender norms, but how Alcaeus's prayer evokes a specific setting and audience, whereas Sappho's prayer situates her poem at the margins of an envisioned ritual occasion (D'Alessio 2018).

This comparison with Alcaeus fr. 129 also highlights a crucial aspect of how Sappho constructs the first-, second-, and third-person roles in this dramatized conversation.[47] In Alcaeus's song, he and his companions ("we") beg the gods ("you") for vengeance against Pittacus ("him"). There is no differentiation between the speaker ("I") and his comrades ("us"). In contrast, Sappho constructs the Brothers Poem as a fictional conversation between the speaker ("I") and her interlocutor

---

legitimate for women." Swift 2018, 84: "[Women] cannot do anything more active than talk or pray [...] Even young girls can offer their prayers, and should be encouraged to do so."

45. Gribble (2016, 59–64) briefly discusses intriguing parallels.

46. See Parker 1993, 343–344, on praying to the gods as poetic, not female activity.

47. I explore other consequences of constructing the song through a dramatized conversation in the following section of this paper.

("you") about Charaxos ("him") through the first two stanzas of the poem (5–12). Then, at line 13, the speaker prays that Charaxos "find us unscathed." This first reference to "us" melds the speaker and her interlocutor, formerly at odds over how to respond to Charaxos's absence, into a cohesive unit.[48] Whereas Alcaeus speaks of himself and his companions only in the first-person plural, Sappho performs the union of 'you-and-me'—fictional interlocutor and speaker, and perhaps by extension audience and singer—into 'us.' Through the formal structure of a dialogue and the content of the prayer, the poem itself enacts the consensus it represents.

To summarize: in the first half of the poem the speaker prays to the gods, invests hope in a third party, and channels her interlocutor's misplaced anxiety toward a mutual goal. Sappho thus drew on what I have called the poetics of misfortune to model a reconciliation between two people in disagreement over how to confront their plight.

After 'Sappho' urges the appropriate course of action to ensure her family's safety, in the second half of the poem she suggests how she and her interlocutor should handle the rest (13–24):

> τὰ δ' ἄλλα
> πάντα δαιμόνεσσιν ἐπιτρόπωμεν·
> εὔδιαι γὰρ ἐκ μεγάλαν ἀήταν   15
>   αἶψα πέλονται.
> τῶν κε βόλληται βασίλευς Ὀλύμπω
> δαίμον' ἐκ πόνων ἐπάρωγον ἤδη
> περτρόπην, κῆνοι μάκαρες πέλονται
>   καὶ πολύολβοι.   20
> κἄμμες, αἴ κε ϝὰν κεφάλαν ἀέρρη
> Λάριχος καὶ δή ποτ' ἄνηρ γένηται,
> καὶ μάλ' ἐκ πόλλαν βαρυθυμίαν κεν
>   αἶψα λύθειμεν.

>   But as for the rest
> let's entrust everything to the gods;
> for fair weather after great storms
>   soon comes.
> Whom the king of Olympus wishes
> a helper spirit to divert from their toils,
> those people become blessed

---

48. Kurke (2016, 248–249) argues that the shift to "a unified and harmonious 'we'" within the Brothers Poem takes place through the "proper activity and content of prayer."

and very wealthy.
We too, if Larichos raises his head
and becomes a man one day,
truly from many burdens of the heart
we would soon be released.

Just as Alcaeus fr. 129 and Sappho fr. 5 shift from a prayer for immediate safety to wishes for the future around the midpoint of the poem (τὸν Ὕρραον δὲ παῖδα, 13; γένοιτο δ' ἄμμι, 7), here the Brothers Poem shifts from prayers for safety to "everything else" (τὰ δ' ἄλλα, 13), that is, the full ship and everything it represents: not just mere survival, but good fortune and future prosperity.[49] 'Sappho' advocates turning over the issue of prosperity to the gods. Why? Good weather follows storms, Zeus can help people become wealthy if he wants a helpful *daimon* to save them from their troubles, and "we too" might be freed from misery if Larichos one day becomes a man.[50]

As in the first half of the poem, some of Sappho's diction in this second half is unusual: the syntax of the conditional relative clause at lines 17–19 (starting with τῶν κε [...]) is contorted, and ἐπιτρόπωμεν at line 14 may be the only hortatory subjunctive in Sappho's extant poetry, though both these constructions appear in Alcaeus.[51] Lidov (2016, 105) interprets these features as further evidence of the Brothers Poem's "awkward" persona and "non-poetic quality." Again, I would be inclined rather to hear an echo of the exhortations Alcaeus delivered at the symposium. For example, in fr. 6, Alcaeus urges on his companions with several hortatory subjunctives: "Let's fortify [the ship?]" (φαρξώμεθ', 7); "Let's race to a safe harbor" (δρό[μωμεν, 8); and "Let's not disgrace our noble ancestors" (μὴ καταισχύνωμεν, 13)."[52] Fr. 6, along with other ship-of-state poems, is often read as political allegory concealing a message for Alcaeus's *hetaireia*, the fictional sailors addressed in the first-person plural. Yet far from encoding military stratagems or political ploys, such exhortations simply aim to remove any reluctance (ὄκνος

---

49. Ferrari 2014, 3–4. See also Euripides, *Alc.* 788–789: "Consider your daily subsistence in your hands; *the rest* is up to fate" (τὸν καθ' ἡμέραν / βίον λογίζου σόν, **τὰ δ' ἄλλα** τῆς τύχης).

50. The image of Larichos "becoming a man [ἄνηρ] one day" (22) may draw on male aristocratic discourse (e.g., Alcaeus fr. 112.10: ἄνδρες γὰρ πόλιος πύργος ἀρεύιοι ["for warlike men are a city's bulwark"]); see also Obbink 2014b, 35.

51. Lidov 2016, 103. I have identified possibly two additional hortatory subjunctives in Sappho's corpus:]νώμεθ' ὀ[(fr. 83.3), and θύω[με]ν Ἀφροδ[ίτηι (Page *SLG* 286 = P.Mich. inv. 3498, recto, col. ii, line 13), an incipit that Page (1974, 97) tentatively assigns to Anacreon, but which I suggest could belong to Sappho. The verb ἐπιτρέπειν is used in a similar vein in Alcaeus's poetry: "There is no need to turn over [ἐπιτρέπην] one's heart to troubles" (335.1).

52. In fr. 346 he simply tells his friends, "Let's drink!" (πώνωμεν, 1).

μόλθ[ακος, 9) and spur one's comrades to collective action. The goal of these directives to an implied and real audience is to ensure that 'we' are in the right mindset to confront misfortune together.

This, then, is how I would read ἐπιτρόπωμεν in the Brothers Poem: when the speaker proposes entrusting future prosperity to the gods, what matters most is that 'we'—speaker and interlocutor, poet and audience—adopt a mindset that will allow them to face their difficulties together. Indeed, most of the poem focuses on the proper actions and emotional attitudes in response to misfortune. Moreover, when the speaker proposes that 'we' entrust future prosperity to the gods, she is not admitting her own powerlessness. Rather, she represents it as an active decision: "Let's turn everything else over to the gods" (13-14). In the following lines, the maxim that good weather follows "gales" (ἀήταν, 15) may even employ the same maritime imagery that Alcaeus uses in fr. 249: giving advice about seafaring, he appears to say that "It is better not to restrain gales [ἀήταις]" (4-5) and later that "[One must go wherever?] the wind carries" (11).[53] Even in a vulnerable situation, it was possible to represent resignation to one's circumstances using the language of activity and agency.

Finally, there remains one, more striking resemblance between the Brothers Poem and Alcaeus's political poetry. As discussed earlier, in fr. 129 Alcaeus uses ῥύεσθαι with (ὐπ)έκ and the genitive twice: first, of the gods saving his companions, and then of his companions saving Mytilene. Sappho uses similar phrasing to similar ends three times in the second half of the Brothers Poem. First we have the gnomic statement that "after great storms, fair weather soon comes" (εὔδιαι γὰρ **ἐκ μεγάλαν ἀήταν αἶψα πέλονται**, 15-16). Then follows a reflection on the gods: whom Zeus wishes to help by sending a helper *daimōn* to "divert them from their troubles, they become blessed and very wealthy" (**ἐκ πόνων** [...] περτρόπην, κῆνοι μάκαρες **πέλονται** καὶ πολύολβοι, 18-20).[54] As in the lines above, ἐκ with the genitive expresses the negative circumstances one hopes will change, and πέλονται denotes what will turn out to be the case. Finally, the speaker connects these gnomic statements to hopes for her own situation: if Larichos becomes a

---

53. See also ἀήται[ς] in Sappho 20.9 and maritime imagery in Alcaeus frr. 6, 73, and 208, the so-called ship-of-state poems. The Brothers Poem's εὔδιαι ("good weather," 15) appears in Pindar, Aeschylus, and other later authors as a metaphor for peace (e.g., Aeschylus, *Sept.* 795-796: πόλις δ' **ἐν εὐδίᾳ** τε καὶ κλυδωνίου / πολλαῖσι πληγαῖς ἄντλον οὐκ ἐδέξατο, also employing a nautical metaphor). Obbink (2015, 9) considers the nautical and weather imagery "part of a repertoire for thinking about the symposium"; see also Stehle 1997, 227. I note that Bierl (2016, 316-317) and Gribble (2016, 51-52) have also suggested Alcaeus's ship of state as a parallel.

54. Compare ῥύεσθαι and ἐκ πόνων in Alcaeus's brother poem, where he says that his brother Antimenidas fought as an ally of the Babylonians and "freed them from troubles" (εὐρύσαο ἐκ πόνων) by killing a colossal warrior (350.4).

man, "truly from many burdens of the heart we would soon be released" (καὶ μάλ' ἐκ πόλλαν βαρυθυμίαν κεν αἶψα λύθειμεν, 23-24). As in the two previous stanzas she uses ἐκ with the genitive, and she repeats αἶψα from the first gnomic statement on fair weather "soon" following storms.

The similarities in phrasing would be striking on their own: both songs express being freed from hardship in similar language and both repeat this phrasing internally to create parallels across stanzas.[55] But even more curious is how repetition in both songs creates implicit parallels between god and man. In Alcaeus fr. 129, the repetition of ῥύεσθαι/(ὑπ)ἐκ/genitive implicitly compared the Olympian gods to Alcaeus's companions. In the Brothers Poem, repetition creates an implicit parallel between the "helpful *daimōn*," which at Zeus's bidding can free people from toils (ἐκ πόνων), and Larichos, whose maturation would free 'us' from despair (ἐκ πόλλαν βαρυθυμίαν).[56] Sappho's implicit comparison between the "helpful *daimōn*" and Larichos paints the speaker's gloomy prospects in a more hopeful light. It suggests that aid often comes about indirectly and rationalizes the speaker's dependence on another.

Despite differing in tone and subject matter, therefore, the Brothers Poem, Alcaeus fr. 129, and other poems by the Lesbian poets frame misfortune using similar vocabulary, structures, imagery, and rhetorical techniques. Some of these formal similarities have been noted by scholars who have also analyzed at length references to the Lesbian triad and Messon sanctuary, and have speculated that the Brothers Poem refers to the political turmoil of Alcaeus's poetry. However, faced with these similarities in form, content, and context, they have described the Brothers Poem and its speaking voice using a critical vocabulary nigh unimaginable for Alcaeus. It is worth reiterating that nothing in the poem identifies the speaker as a woman.[57] If Alcaeus had brothers named Charaxos and Larichos, would we be talking about awkward personae, intimate domestic spheres, young boys offering their prayers, or prudent and submissive men?[58]

Gender certainly is an important factor in any reading of the Brothers Poem, but the parallels explored above caution against overly simplistic gendered or

---

55. Alcaeus fr. 70 also contains striking parallels to the Brothers Poem; cf. fr. 70.7-8 (θᾶς κ' ἄμμε βόλλητ' Ἄρευς [...] / τρόπην) to lines 17-20 of the Brothers Poem (τῶν κε βόλληται βασίλευς Ὀλύμπω [...] περτρόπην); 70.8 (ἐκ δὲ χόλω τῶδε) to the ἐκ + gen. constructions above (15, 18, 23); and the θυμός compound in 70.9 (θυμοβόρω λύας ["strife that devours one's heart"]) to the βαρυθυμίαν ("burdens of the heart") in the final stanza of the Brothers Poem (see also Alcaeus fr. 348.2: βαρυδαίμονος ["ill-fated"]). I am grateful to the anonymous reader who suggested Sappho fr. 1.25-26 (χαλέπαν δὲ λῦσον ἐκ μερίμναν) as another comparandum.

56. See also Mueller 2016, 39.

57. I am grateful to the anonymous reader for suggesting this line of argumentation.

58. See notes 6 and 44 above.

otherwise exceptionalist readings. Only if we accept that the Lesbian poets drew from a shared poetic repertoire can we develop a more nuanced appreciation of what makes Sappho's poetry different. In the next section I explore at greater length how the Brothers Poem, like Sappho's poetry more generally, adapts traditional models so as to highlight women's agency. Though the speaker of the Brothers Poem is in peril, she does not take a passive stance. Rather, she actively enlists the gods' help, pins hope on her brothers, and unites with her interlocutor while the storm rages around them.

II Crafting a Woman-Centered Experience of Misfortune

Let us shift from features shared by Alcaeus and Sappho to a different set of questions. What features does the Brothers Poem share with the rest of Sappho's poetry? What poetic techniques did Sappho employ that were characteristically her own? And how might the Brothers Poem address the women in its audience?

Critics situating the Brothers Poem within Sappho's corpus have tended to focus on the poem's content, namely, its mentions of Charaxos and Larichos, and have accordingly read the poem alongside Sappho's other 'brother poems.'[59] This valuable line of investigation has examined the relationship between biographical persons and lyric personae to explain why a song cycle about named individuals would appeal to those outside the family.[60] The fact that Sappho here sings about her brothers (rather than other women) has also prompted scholars to analyze how Sappho speaks about men from a woman's perspective. They have proposed that the Brothers Poem gives a glimpse into women's domestic sphere, and have explored how the Brothers Poem refashions Homeric epic to highlight the experiences of women.[61] According to these readings, the Brothers Poem gives us a rare glimpse of a sister speaking about her brothers, of a woman singing about men.

---

59. This song cycle included frr. 5 and 15, along with perhaps 3, 7, 9, and 20. On Sappho's 'brother poems' see Boedeker 2016, 194–195; Lardinois 2016; Lidov 2016, 59–87; Obbink 2016b, 50; O'Connell 2018.

60. Nagy 2015, §§ 49–56, and 2016, 489–492; Bär 2016, 13–15; Lardinois 2016, 184–187; Peponi 2016; Stehle 2016, 266–268; also Lidov 2016, 86 note 50, on speaking names.

61. See Kurke 2016 on the view "behind the scenes," Nagy 2016 on the "poetics of sisterly affect," and Peponi 2016 on the "mythopoetics of the domestic." Swift (2018), by analyzing depictions of famous brother-pairs from archaic poetry, argues that the Brothers Poem presents "domestic morality from a different, female-oriented perspective, showing the responsibilities that men bear toward their female dependents" (71). However, Swift concludes that the women in the poem lack agency: the speaker is "powerless" and the women "cannot do anything more active than talk or pray," because "[t]he poem's ending makes it clear that action can be taken to save the family, but neither the speaker nor addressee is capable of doing so" (83–84). In a view closer to my own, Mueller (2016) argues that the Brothers Poem rewrites Odyssean narratives of homecoming from

Such readings have been productive, but I believe a less androcentric reading can illuminate some "woman-centered" aspects of the poem that others have neglected. Drawing on Jack Winkler's and Marilyn Skinner's studies of "double consciousness" and "woman-centeredness" in Sappho's erotic poetry,[62] I argue that the Brothers Poem also centers around women, for, despite its appellation, the poem is not primarily about the brothers. Although the poem mentions Charaxos and Larichos, it dwells far longer on 'us,' the poem's first-person plural, to whom the speaker returns over and over. Although the speaker's brothers are responsible for her misfortune, she focuses not on their failings, but on how she and her interlocutor should confront their circumstances. While the poem engages with Homeric precedents, Sappho telescopes the *Odyssey* and *Telemachy* into the shortest essential units—Odysseus's homecoming, Telemachus's coming of age—and devotes the rest of the poem to the activities of women. In all these ways, the Brothers Poem is typical of Sappho's woman-centered poetry, in particular her erotic poems, with which it shares significant formal features. If, for a moment, we train our attention not on the eponymous brothers but on the speaker and her interlocutor, we can explore what the poem might have communicated to the women in Sappho's audience.

Before we dive into the Brothers Poem, I would like to propose an identity, or at least a gender, for the unnamed interlocutor. The identity of the interlocutor is crucial for interpreting the poem's depiction of agency and gender relations, and scholars have accordingly scrutinized the poem for clues. We need someone close enough to Sappho's family to be concerned about Charaxos's return, yet someone who might prize economic interests (the "full ship") over his safety; someone who could be described as babbling and who would take instruction from Sappho, but who might also send Sappho to pray to Hera.[63] Based on these objective criteria, most scholars have reasoned that the likeliest candidate is Sappho's mother.[64] Yet their reasons for viewing the interlocutor as a woman (or a man) often depend so greatly on normative ideas about gender and agency that these internal criteria are insufficient evidence on their own.[65]

---

a woman's perspective, and concludes that "the female speaker exercises voice and agency in relation to the *nostos* of a male relative" (43). I find less compelling her mapping of genre onto gender, according to which the Brothers Poem metapoetically opposes "a distinctively lyric type of *nostos*" to male epic (28). Notably, none of these studies consider a female audience.

62. Winkler 1981 and Skinner 1993; additional bibliography in note 11 above.

63. See note 4 above for bibliography.

64. Although other candidates have been proposed: Sappho's father, her brothers Larichos or E(u)rigios, her daughter, an uncle, a servant, a nurse, or even Charaxos's mistress or spouse. Neri (2015, 58–59) concisely lists the possible interlocutors with relevant bibliography.

65. E.g., Kurke (2016), discussing the verb θρύλησθα, finds it "almost impossible to believe that Sappho is addressing a man, using this verb to characterize his speech" (239); similarly, Swift (2018, 83–84) states that the verb "suggests the useless chatter stereotypically associated with

Barring the fortuitous discovery of the poem's opening lines, I do not think it will be possible to settle exactly who the interlocutor is. However, one criterion external to the Brothers Poem makes a strong case that the interlocutor is a woman: except in wedding songs, Sappho never addresses a man. In poem after poem, she speaks to and recalls conversations with women—her lovers, friends, enemies, and family members.[66] But never does she bestow her words on a man, nor do the words of men intrude in her songs. The Brothers Poem is not a wedding song; in fact, as I discuss below, the conversational setting is similar to that of many other songs in which Sappho addresses a woman, thereby offering her female audience a world populated by the perspectives, activities, and emotions of women. At this stage I simply ask the reader to entertain the idea that the interlocutor is a woman, and to see how this dynamic plays out.

The first technique to examine is how Sappho constructs the dramatic setting. By staging the Brothers Poem as a fictional conversation between two women, Sappho blurs the line between the world of her song and the world of her audience. This is the same framing device that Sappho uses in fr. 98b, a poem that also interweaves family, wealth, and politics.[67] The poem is fragmentary, but it clearly refers to "the exile of the Cleanactid(s?)" (τὰς Κλεανακτιδα[/ φύγας, 8–9), the clan of the infamous tyrant Myrsilus, and "the Mytilenean" (τὼι Μυτιληνάωι, 3), perhaps Myrsilus or Pittacus. In the poem 'Sappho' may be telling Cleis, her mother or her daughter, that she once possessed elegant accessories when the Cleanactids were in exile.[68] Now that the Cleanactids are back in power, their family can no longer buy costly headbands—not just girlish accessories, but meaningful symbols of former affluence, now lost.[69]

We can analyze fr. 98b as political, both in terms of the content internal to the fictional song-world (two women discussing their impoverishment in connection to political turmoil), and when we consider its real-world context (an audience that included women affected by politics). Within the song, 'Sappho' explains to Cleis

---

women." Meanwhile for Bierl (2016), the interlocutor is a man who "represents a strictly male view, secular and more superficial, economically based," against which Sappho adopts "a traditional and typically female position" (330–331).

66. This applies to divinities as well. In her songs she addresses female goddesses such as Aphrodite, Hera, Nereids, Muses, etc. The only possible exception I can find is fr. 95.8, where she addresses someone, possibly Hermes, as "ὦ δέσποτ'."

67. See Caciagli 2016, 437–441, for a reading of fr. 98b similar to my own.

68. As Page (1955, 102–103) argues, though the poem is too fragmentary to be certain. Other interpretations have been proposed, most recently by Ferrari 2010, 1–18, who contends that Sappho was a member of the Cleanactids.

69. Williamson (1995, 85–86) and Parker (2005, 13) discuss beauty and dress as symbols of social class in Sappho, Theognis, Anacreon, and Semonides. See also Kurke 1992 on luxury as an aristocratic ideal.

that their family faces difficulties because their enemies are in power. At the same time, Sappho-as-singer voices concerns about the repercussions of political strife on women, a matter all-too-familiar to female audiences in archaic Mytilene and beyond. By portraying these issues through a dramatized conversation between women and by addressing her words to a second-person "you," Sappho encourages women in her audience to hear the speaker's words for Cleis as words for herself. Moreover, by adding a second female character (Cleis) to the scenario, Sappho offers an additional perspective for women to adopt.[70] Fr. 98b reminds her perhaps of a time when she too had to tell a loved one why the purse strings were tighter, or had heard the same.

So too in the Brothers Poem: within the song-world, 'Sappho' speaks about her unavailing brothers and her family's resulting hardship. These issues—dependence on male relatives, loss of social status, the threat of impoverishment or worse—mirrored the experiences of her female audience members. Furthermore, framing the poem as a fictional conversation between women encouraged audience members to envision themselves in the conversation, whether as the recipient of Sappho's words or by adopting the perspective of one of the female characters. The odd timescale in the Brothers Poem further blurs the boundary between the here-and-now of her audience and the then-and-there of her song, which, unlike most of Sappho's longer fragments, lacks past tense verbs. When the speaker says "you are always chattering" (ἄï θρύλησθα) in the present tense, she merges the time and place of her interlocutor's endless chattering with those of her performance.[71]

To return to fr. 98b one last time: despite my focus on its political content, it is important to note that the fragment is not solely concerned with the public sphere. What makes the song, even in its tattered state, so compelling is the way the world outside the home merges with the world within through an object: a lovely headband—or rather the memory of a lovely headband, which symbolizes everything they have lost. We might call fr. 98b the "Mitra Poem" insofar as it is 'about' a headband, but this object is also a means of exploring material loss, family obligations, and politics, topics that span the spheres of civic and domestic, public and intimate. I interpret Charaxos and Larichos in the Brothers Poem in a similar fashion: as figures on whom to pin hopes and memories, and as a means of singing about family and politics, hardship and prosperity, divine omnipotence and human limitation. Interpretations that impose a binary opposition between male/public and female/private on the Brothers Poem tend to obscure how tightly these issues

---

70. See Winkler 1981 on double-consciousness and multiple perspectives in Sappho's poetry.
71. The adverb ἄï is shockingly rare in Lesbian poetry. I count only two instances: Sappho 44Aa.5: ἄï πάρθενος ἔσσομαι (or the compound adjective ἀïπάρθενος), and 44.6: ἀïννάω. Yet there is no other word the Lesbian poets use to express "always/ever/constantly."

are interwoven through Sappho's focus on collective responsibility. Thus, the dramatic framework of the Brothers Poem allows Sappho to sing about her audience's concerns at a remove, speak to them through a fictional addressee, craft female characters with different perspectives, and explore all this through the brothers.

Now I would like to delve into the conversation between Sappho and her interlocutor to examine its dynamics, dynamics that I believe critics have not fully understood. At lines 4–13, 'Sappho' chastises her interlocutor for babbling about Charaxos coming with a full ship; instead she ought to send Sappho to pray to Hera that Charaxos arrive steering a *safe* ship—and that he find them unharmed. In subtly reworking her interlocutor's speech, Sappho takes on a didactic role within the conversational framework.[72] This is the same technique she uses in fr. 94, in which she describes to her audience how she consoled a woman forced to leave her. Her departing companion said in tears (4–5): "Ah, what *awful things we've suffered* [δεῖνα πεπ[όνθ]αμεν]. Sappho, truly I'm leaving you against my will." Sappho's fragmentary reply follows (7–11): "Farewell, go, and remember me, since you know how we cared for you. But if not, still I want to remind you [...] what [soft] and *beautiful things we experienced* [κάλ' ἐπάσχομεν]." Winkler's reading superbly captures the dynamics of this scene: "The departing woman says δεῖνα πεπόνθαμεν, 'fearful things we have suffered,' and Sappho corrects her, κάλ' ἐπάσχομεν, 'beautiful things we continuously experienced.'"[73] To make explicit what Winkler's translation and analysis bring out implicitly, Sappho corrects not just the qualitative description of their experiences together (δεῖνα, κάλ') but the timescale: the perfect tense of the woman's πεπόνθαμεν sullies the past with the immediate pain of separation, whereas Sappho's ἐπάσχομεν in the imperfect safeguards the beautiful memories of what they shared together—habitually ("we used to"), iteratively ("again and again"), but no more.[74]

In the Brothers Poem, 'Sappho' adopts a similar didactic role when she corrects her interlocutor, who inappropriately babbles about Charaxos returning with a "full" ship. Leslie Kurke (2016, 240–241) comments suggestively that, in addition to correcting the content ("full" to "safe"), the speaker also corrects the *manner* of her interlocutor's speech from babbling (θρύλησθα) to prayer (λίσσεσθαι). To build on Kurke's reading, I would add that the speaker also corrects her interlocu-

---

72. Not in the sense of "pedagogical," but simply as an archaic lyric poet giving instruction.

73. Winkler 1981, 84. See also McEvilley 1971 on the effect of repetition and metrical responsion across stanzas; Williamson 1995, 148–149, on the multiplicity of perspectives that Sappho offers her female audience; Greene 1994, 44–48, and Wilson 1996, 128, on how the 'I/you' mode switches to a 'we' mode that gradually encompasses all audience members; and Stehle 1997, 310, on "resistance to emotional passivity."

74. O'Connell (2018, 240–243) discusses the "poetics of correction" in Sappho's Brothers Poem, fr. 94, and fr. 137 within the framework of archaic songs of welcome.

tor's *behavior*. What the interlocutor should do is stop babbling and "thinking" (νόησθαι), and instead "send and order" the speaker (πέμπην ἔμε καὶ κέλεσθαι). Metrical responsion and the repetition of ἀλλά at the beginning of both stanzas (**ἀλλ᾽** ἄϊ θρύλησθα Χάραξον ἔλθην, 5; **ἀλλὰ** καὶ πέμπην ἔμε καὶ κέλεσθαι, 9) underscore the contrast between babbling and taking action. Thus, the correction is not primarily from one manner of speech to another, but from a passive attitude (babbling, thinking) to an active response (sending, ordering). If the interlocutor's manner of speaking does stand to be corrected, as Kurke suggests, I would say that the alternative to useless babbling is the efficacious speech-act of "sending and ordering" Sappho to pray. Debates over which family member would have the authority to send Sappho, or why Sappho is the one who prays to Hera, have overlooked this fundamental dynamic. In Sappho's correction, both women have agency and they act together. Thus, in Sappho's didactic mode she encourages "you"—her interlocutor, and by extension the women in her audience—to eschew passive suffering and instead take collective action.

In addition to correcting her interlocutor's passive behavior, the speaker also corrects her interlocutor's image of Charaxos's behavior: that "Charaxos *come with* a full ship" (Χάραξον **ἔλθην** / νᾶϊ **σὺν** πλήαι). The speaker instead hopes that "Charaxos *arrive here* steering a safe ship" (**ἐξίκεσθαι τυίδε** σάαν ἄγοντα | νᾶα Χάραξον). In her rephrasing Charaxos should be steering the ship actively rather than accompanying it passively. Moreover, she exchanges the bland ἔλθην ("come") for the expanded ἐξίκεσθαι τυίδε ("arrive here"), indicating a completed journey and reorienting the scene around the speaker and interlocutor. I suggest that the speaker's vision of Charaxos steering his ship "here" complements the identification of Charaxos with Odysseus within the Homeric *nostos*-motif that others have explored.[75]

The *nostos*-motif is fully activated by the second part of the prayer: that Charaxos also "find us unscathed" (κάμμ᾽ **ἐπεύρην ἀρτέμεας**, 13). As others have noted, the rare word ἀρτεμής, coupled with the verb εὑρίσκω, appears in Book 13 of the *Odyssey*. Before leaving Phaeacia, Odysseus prays that he will find his wife and his loved ones safe at home upon his return: ἀμύμονα δ᾽ οἴκοι ἄκοιτιν / νοστήσας **εὕροιμι** σὺν **ἀρτεμέεσσι** φίλοισιν (13.42–43).[76] In the Brothers Poem, Sappho activates the Homeric paradigm of Odysseus finding his loved ones "unscathed" as a structural and intertextual parallel for Charaxos finding his family "unscathed." Furthermore, as some scholars (e.g., Bär 2016, 24–25, and Mueller

---

75. See esp. Nünlist 2014; Bär 2016, 23–27; Kurke 2016, 249–251; Mueller 2016; Stehle 2016, 275–277.

76. Nünlist 2014, 13, and Kurke 2016, 250. The word ἀρτεμής is attested only three times in archaic poetry, once in the *Odyssey*, as noted above, and twice in the *Iliad* (5.515, 7.308).

2016) have astutely observed, by praying that Charaxos find "us" (rather than "his family") unscathed, Sappho reorients this Odyssean precedent around Penelope's perspective. Thus, critics have interpreted κἄμμ' ἐπεύρην ἀρτέμεας as a textual pointer to a Homeric model, refashioned from a woman's perspective.

Surely this is right, but the heightened tone of ἀρτεμής and its enjambment suggest that we should read κἄμμ' ἐπεύρην ἀρτέμεας not merely as a mythic citation. Within the poem's fiction, whatever peril Charaxos faces at sea, the poetic 'we' is in even greater danger.[77] The nature and source of this danger are not specified, but Sappho's aristocratic audience might well have imagined a range of possibilities: losing one's property, facing exile, or even risking one's life, as ἀρτεμής implies.[78] Therefore, I believe the closing line of the speaker's prayer does two things. First, it shifts attention from Charaxos and his sea voyage to 'us,' the women who are in true danger.[79] Charaxos, like an elegant headband, has been the topic of conversation, but he is not the real focus; rather, he provides an opportunity for singing about the actions, emotional attitudes, and wellbeing of women. Second, by activating Penelope's perspective at the moment when the speaker shifts focus to 'us,' Sappho forges a powerful link between the mythic world of Penelope's *Odyssey*, the fictional song-world of 'Sappho' and her interlocutor, and the here-and-now of the poet and her female audience.

All of these techniques—endowing women with agency, adapting Homeric epic with sensitivity to the experiences of women, and introducing men only to discard them for the true focus on women—are characteristic of Sappho's poetic repertoire.[80] For example, in the priamel of fr. 16, Sappho sets out what men find most beautiful (cavalry, infantry, navy) as a foil for her own view that the most beautiful thing is whatever one desires.[81] She then introduces Helen as a mythological exemplum, and here one might expect the most beautiful woman in the world to figure as the object of Paris's desire. Instead, Helen is the agent of desire and she evidences Sappho's claim because *she* left behind her husband, child, and parents to

---

77. Liberman 2014, 7; see also Gribble 2016, 43–44, and Lardinois 2016, 176–177.

78. In the *Iliad*, ἀρτεμής describes Aeneas and Hector returning safely after nearly perishing in battle (5.515, 7.308).

79. The emotional crescendo from the bland σάος to the rich ἀρτεμής underscores the shift in focus; see also Stehle 2016, 274.

80. See also fr. 31, in which "that man" initially seems to be the speaker's focus, but is only godlike insofar as he sits across from the woman who is both agent and object of desire: Stehle 1997, 293–294. Winkler (1981, 75–78) argues that fr. 31 adapts Nausicaa's portrayal in *Odyssey* 6. On Sappho fr. 1, see Cameron 1939, Stanley 1976, and Winkler 1981, 68–73 (on agency and the adaptation of *Iliad* 5), with Rissman 1983 on Sappho's "Homericity" in fr. 1 and elsewhere.

81. Winkler 1981, 73–74: "Her proposition is not that men value military forces whereas she values desire, but rather that all valuation is an act of desire."

go to Troy (Stehle 1990, 109–112). Similarly, in the Brothers Poem these techniques allow women to experience their hardship through the fictional world of song and the mythical world of the *Odyssey*. They privilege women's experiences of suffering as equally important to those of men, in a world where family and society created mutual dependencies among women and men alike.

Until line 12 'Sappho' has spoken in the 'I-you' mode that allowed her to address her fictional interlocutor and by extension her audience didactically. With Sappho's prayer for "our" safety in line 13, she transitions to the 'we' mode that characterizes the rest of the song: "*Let's turn* everything else over to the gods" (13–14), and "*We too* [...] *we might be released* from our heavy-heartedness" (21–24).[82] In the 'we' mode, both speaker and interlocutor, formerly at odds, are fused into a single pronominal unit. But 'we' can also encompass Sappho's audience. Indeed, the gnomic reflections that follow (good weather can follow storms, Zeus can turn around someone's life if he chooses) encourage audience members to apply these maxims to their own situations. Just as the fictional interlocutor might take comfort in the speaker's advice, so too could Sappho's audience find companionship and solace in Sappho's song.[83]

Toward the end of the song, we hear about a second brother, Larichos, whom the speaker hopes will grow up one day. Many critics have interpreted the entire second half of the poem (13–24), tightly interwoven as it is through verbal repetition and situational echoes, as culminating in the hopes for Larichos in the final stanza.[84] Yet I would contend that Larichos, much like Charaxos in the first half of the song, is not the true focus. The final stanza begins with κἄμμες ("we too," 21), boldly fronted and cut off from its proper syntactical unit, which comes in the last two lines. The position and hyperbaton of κἄμμες (21) at the beginning of the final stanza are as striking as the position and enjambment of κἄμμ' ἐπεύρην ἀρτέμεας at the beginning of the third stanza (13). Here, κἄμμες (21) reiterates that 'we' are the song's focus. This is what the rest of the clause, delayed until the final two lines, emphasizes: "Truly from many burdens of the heart we would soon be released" (καὶ μάλ' ἐκ πόλλαν βαρυθυμίαν κεν / αἶψα λύθειμεν, 23–24). Echoing κἄμμες (21) with καὶ μάλ' (23), the final lines emphasize the anguish of the first-person plural and the possibility of relief. At the close of the song, 'we'— speaker, interlocutor, singer, audience—remain the subject.

---

82. Cf. the shifts in frr. 5 (ἄμμι, 7) and 94 (πεδήπομεν, 8; ἐπάσχομεν, 11; [ἄμ]μες ἀπέσκομεν, 26).

83. Gribble (2016, 50), reading the poem biographically, suggests that 'we' included the audience because they empathized with Sappho and were personally invested in Charaxos's fate.

84. E.g., Bierl 2016, 314–315; Kurke 2016, 241; Lidov 2016, 105; Stehle 2016.

Conclusion

Gender undoubtedly plays an important role in Sappho's Brothers Poem. Yet a normative conception of gender roles does not fully explain the poem's diction or internal dynamics and may lead us to neglect formal aspects of the poem typical of Sappho's woman-centered poetics. I have argued that Sappho endowed her poem's speaker with agency in the face of hardship using a poetics of misfortune that she shared with Alcaeus. Furthermore, I explored the song's dramatic setting, marginalization of men, and restaging of Homeric myth as characteristic of Sappho's woman-centered erotic poetry.

Decades after the feminist scholarship that first drew attention to how idiosyncratic treatments of Sappho isolated her from other lyric poets, Sappho still meets with a double standard. In this article I have demonstrated the benefits of approaching Sappho first and foremost as a lyric poet before resorting to gender to explain her poetry. It is telling that, in a poem so obviously stripped of erotic coloring, one still encounters the obsession with sex that framed reactions to Sappho's poetry in the twentieth century.[85] This shows that many scholars have still not fully grappled with whether and how Sappho's biographical tradition and reception—with their comic distortions, late anachronisms, and masculinist interpretations of female sexuality—should inform readings of her poetry. In the coming years, these issues will continue to be relevant. As we await a critical edition of Sappho's work that incorporates the newest fragments, how will editors choose whether to assign disputed fragments to Sappho or Alcaeus and what supplements to print?[86] And as scholars reassess Sappho's pragmatics and performance contexts, extrapolating from poetic text to historical setting, they must take into account the similarities to Alcaeus's poetry and give a better methodological justification before inventing different performance occasions for Sappho.

Alcaeus's songs are not just about politics; they *are* politics.[87] Can we be certain that Sappho's songs are not, simply because she was a woman? The available evidence suggests that aristocratic women in archaic Lesbos enjoyed relatively high status, formed social groups based on familial and political ties, and could gain recognition as skilled musicians.[88] In this context they developed a poetic tradition

---

85. See, e.g., Bierl 2016 and Lardinois 2016 on Charaxos's surrender to "the erotic fascination of a beautiful prostitute," Sappho's jealousy over her brother's romance, her inability to rely on Larichos who as a young wine-pourer is "captured in the net of erotic affairs," and the notion that the Brothers Poem functioned as advice to unmarried girls about ideal bridegrooms.

86. E.g., where to include Sappho 99 LP = Alcaeus 303a V, or whether to print Δ]ωριχα in fr. 15.11.

87. Williamson 1995, 71–72: "His poems do not simply reflect political intrigue: they are one of the ways of engaging in it."

88. Friedrich 1978, 108–111, and Wilson 1996, 6. Williamson (1995, 84–86) attributes the lack

that comprehended androcentric language without being restricted to it (Winkler 1981, 70–71). Naturally the 'brothers' have dominated discussions of Sappho's Brothers Poem, and some have concluded that the song illustrates the limitations on women's agency. Yet the Brothers Poem bears the hallmarks of a poet who was sensitive to traditional masculine discourse that denied agency and subjectivity to women, but who refused to replicate it. The poem treats binary oppositions—of action and inaction, of polis and family, of divine omnipotence and human limitation—but does not align them with male or female. Instead, Sappho brought to bear the full range of her poetic repertoire to bend Alcaeus's political arena, the exploits of Charaxos and Larichos, and Odysseus's adventures at sea around a world with women at its core. A woman-centered reading of the Brothers Poem thus allows us to appreciate fully how Sappho drew on poetic tradition, mythic heritage, and her experiences as a woman to speak to her audience over two millennia ago.[89]

Bibliographical References

Aloni, Antonio. 1997. *Saffo, Frammenti*. Firenze: Giunti Editore.
Bär, Silvio. 2016. "'Ceci n'est pas un fragment': Identity, Intertextuality and Fictionality in Sappho's 'Brothers Poem.'" *SO* 90: 8–54.
Benelli, Luca. 2017. *Sapphostudien zu ausgewählten Fragmenten; Teil I*. Paderborn: Ferdinand Schöningh.
Bettenworth, Anja. 2014. "Sapphos Amme: Ein Beitrag zum neuen Sapphofragment (Brothers Poem)." *ZPE* 191: 15–19.
Bierl, Anton. 2016. "'All You Need is Love': Some Thoughts on the Structure, Texture, and Meaning of the Brothers Song as well as on Its Relation to the Kypris Song (P.Sapph.Obbink)." In Bierl and Lardinois 2016, 302–336.
Bierl, Anton, and André Lardinois, eds. 2016. *The Newest Sappho: P.Sapph.Obbink and P. GC inv. 105, frs. 1–4*. Leiden and Boston: Brill.
Boedeker, Deborah. 2016. "Hera and the Return of Charaxos." In Bierl and Lardinois 2016, 188–207.
Boterf, Nicholas. 2018. "Carving Out a Space: Oaths and Spatialization in Alcaeus 129 V." *CP* 113: 381–403.
Budelmann, Felix, and Tom Phillips. 2018a. "Introduction." In Budelmann and Phillips 2018b, 1–27.
Budelmann, Felix, and Tom Phillips, eds. 2018b. *Textual Events: Performance and the Lyric in Early Greece*. Oxford: Oxford University Press.

---

of misogyny in Sappho's poetry in part to her membership in a social class that valued women, and discusses poetic skill as a "badge of social accomplishment for aristocratic women."

89. This article is dedicated to the memory of Albert Henrichs (1942–2017), who read the first draft in 2015 and is dearly missed. MANY thanks (as Albert would say) to David Elmer, Renaud Gagné, Sarah Magagna, Alexander Schwennicke, Richard Thomas, Tim Whitmarsh, and anonymous referees. The remaining errors are my own.

Burnett, Anne. 1983. *Three Archaic Poets: Archilochus, Alcaeus, Sappho.* Cambridge, MA: Harvard University Press.
Caciagli, Stefano. 2011. *Poeti e società: comunicazione poetica e formazioni sociali nella Lesbo del VII/VI secolo a.C.* Amsterdam: Hakkert.
Caciagli, Stefano. 2016. "Sappho Fragment 17: Wishing Charaxos a Safe Trip?" In Bierl and Lardinois 2016, 424–448.
Calame, Claude. 1977. *Les chœurs de jeunes filles en Grèce archaïque, 1: Morphologie, fonction religieuse et sociale; 2: Alcman.* Roma: Edizioni dell'Ateneo e Bizzari.
Cameron, Archibald. 1939. "Sappho's Prayer to Aphrodite." *HTR* 32: 1–17.
Campbell, David. 1967. *Greek Lyric Poetry: A Selection of Early Greek Lyric, Elegiac and Iambic Poetry.* London: Macmillan.
Cantarella, Eva. 1992. *Bisexuality in the Ancient World.* New Haven: Yale University Press.
D'Alessio, Giambattista. 2009. "Language and Pragmatics." In Felix Budelmann, ed., *The Cambridge Companion to Greek Lyric*, 114–129. Cambridge: Cambridge University Press.
D'Alessio, Giambattista. 2018. "Fiction and Pragmatics in Ancient Greek Lyric: The Case of Sappho." In Budelmann and Phillips 2018b, 31–62.
DeJean, Joan. 1989. "Sex and Philology: Sappho and the Rise of German Nationalism." *Representations* 27: 148–171.
Donlan, Walter. 1985. "Pistos Philos Hetairos." In Thomas Figueira and Gregory Nagy, eds., *Theognis of Megara: Poetry and the Polis*, 223–244. Baltimore: Johns Hopkins University Press.
Elmer, David. 2013. "Poetry's Politics in Archaic Greek Epic and Lyric." *Oral Tradition* 28: 143–166.
Ferrari, Franco. 2010. *Sappho's Gift: The Poet and Her Community.* Ann Arbor: University of Michigan Press.
Ferrari, Franco. 2014. "Saffo e i suoi fratelli e altri brani del primo libro." *ZPE* 192: 1–19.
Friedrich, Paul. 1978. *The Meaning of Aphrodite.* Chicago: University of Chicago Press.
Gagné, Renaud. 2013. *Ancestral Fault in Ancient Greece.* Cambridge: Cambridge University Press.
Gentili, Bruno. 1988. *Poetry and its Public in Ancient Greece: From Homer to the Fifth Century.* Baltimore: Johns Hopkins University Press.
Greene, Ellen. 1994. "Apostrophe and Women's Erotics in the Poetry of Sappho." *TAPA* 124: 41–56.
Greene, Ellen. 2008. "Masculine and Feminine, Public and Private, in the Poetry of Sappho." In Jacob Blevins, ed., *Dialogism and Lyric Self-Fashioning: Bakhtin and the Voices of a Genre*, 23–45. Selinsgrove, PA: Susquehanna University Press.
Gribble, David. 2016. "Getting Ready to Pray: Sappho's New 'Brothers' Song." *G&R* 63: 29–68.
Hallett, Judith. 1979. "Sappho and Her Social Context: Sense and Sensuality." *Signs* 4: 447–464.
Henrichs, Albert. 2014. "What's in a Prayer? Sappho's Way with Words." Paper delivered at Bard College, October 2014. Provided by author.
Higgins, Charlotte. 2020. "A Scandal in Oxford: The Curious Case of the Stolen Gospel." *The Guardian.* 9 January 2020. https://www.theguardian.com/news/2020/jan/09/a-scandal-in-oxford-the-curious-case-of-the-stolen-gospel. (accessed 22 October 2021)
Hunter, Richard, and Anna Uhlig. 2017. "Introduction: What Is Reperformance?" In Richard Hunter and Anna Uhlig, eds., *Imagining Reperformance in Ancient Culture: Studies in the Traditions of Drama and Lyric*, 1–17. Cambridge: Cambridge University Press.
Konstan, David. 1997. *Friendship in the Classical World.* Cambridge: Cambridge University Press.
Kurke, Leslie. 1992. "The Politics of ἁβροσύνη in Archaic Greece." *CA* 11: 91–120.

Kurke, Leslie. 1994. "Crisis and Decorum in Sixth-Century Lesbos: Reading Alkaios Otherwise." *QUCC* 47: 67–92.
Kurke, Leslie. 2016. "Gendered Spheres and Mythic Models in Sappho's Brothers Poem." In Bierl and Lardinois 2016, 238–265.
Lardinois, André. 1994. "Subject and Circumstance in Sappho's Poetry." *TAPA* 124: 57–84.
Lardinois, André. 2010. "Lesbian Sappho Revisited." In Jitse Dijkstra, Justin Kroesen, and Yme Kuiper, eds., *Myths, Martyrs, and Modernity: Studies in the History of Religions in Honour of Jan N. Bremmer*, 13–30. Leiden and Boston: Brill.
Lardinois, André. 2016. "Sappho's Brothers Song and the Fictionality of Early Greek Lyric Poetry." In Bierl and Lardinois 2016, 167–187.
Lefkowitz, Mary. 1973. "Critical Stereotypes and the Poetry of Sappho." *GRBS* 14: 113–123.
Liberman, Gautier. 2014. "Reflections on a New Poem by Sappho concerning Her Anguish and Her Brothers." English translation by Paul Ellis. Paper delivered at F.I.E.C. Bordeaux, August 2014. www.papyrology.ox.ac.uk/Fragments/Liberman.FIEC.Bordeaux.2014.pdf. (accessed 15 October 2021)
Lidov, Joel. 2002. "Sappho, Herodotus, and the Hetaira." *CP* 97: 203–237.
Lidov, Joel. 2016. "Songs for Sailors and Lovers." In Bierl and Lardinois 2016, 55–109.
Mazza, Roberta. 2020. "News on the Newest Sappho Fragments: Back to Christie's Salerooms." *Faces & Voices* (blog). 13 January 2020. https://facesandvoices.wordpress.com/2020/01/13/news-on-the-newest-sappho-fragments-back-to-christies-salerooms/. (accessed 22 October 2021)
McEvilley, Thomas. 1971. "Sappho, Fragment Ninety-Four." *Phoenix* 25: 1–11.
Merkelbach, Reinhold. 1957. "Sappho und ihr Kreis." *Philologus* 101: 1–29.
Most, Glenn. 1982. "Greek Lyric Poets." In T. James Luce, ed., *Ancient Writers: Greece and Rome; Vol. 1: Homer to Caesar*, 75–98. New York: Charles Scribners Sons.
Mueller, Melissa. 2016. "Re-Centering Epic *Nostos*: Gender and Genre in Sappho's Brothers Poem." *Arethusa* 49: 25–46.
Nagy, Gregory. 2007. "Did Sappho and Alcaeus Ever Meet? Symmetries of Myth and Ritual in Performing the Songs of Ancient Lesbos." In Anton Bierl, Rebecca Lämmle, and Katharina Wesselmann, eds., *Literatur und Religion: Wege zu einer mythisch-rituellen Poetik bei den Griechen*, 211–269. Berlin: Walter De Gruyter.
Nagy, Gregory. 2015. "Genre, Occasion, and Choral Mimesis Revisited—with Special Reference to the 'Newest Sappho.'" *Classical Inquiries*. 1 October 2015. https://classical-inquiries.chs.harvard.edu/genre-occasion-and-choral-mimesis-revisited-with-special-reference-to-the-newest-sappho/. (accessed 22 October 2021)
Nagy, Gregory. 2016. "A Poetics of Sisterly Affect in the Brothers Song and in Other Songs of Sappho." In Bierl and Lardinois 2016, 449–492.
Neri, Camillo. 2015. "Il *Brothers Poem* e l'edizione alessandrina (in margine a *P.Sapph.Obbink*)." *Eikasmos* 26: 53–76.
Nongbri, Brent. 2019. "Dirk Obbink, Scott Carroll, and Sappho." *Variant Readings* (blog). 3 August 2019. https://brentnongbri.com/2019/08/03/dirk-obbink-scott-carroll-and-sappho/. (accessed 22 October 2021)
Nünlist, René. 2014. "Das Schiff soll unversehrt sein, nicht voll! Zu Sapphos neuem Lied über die Brüder." *ZPE* 191: 13–14.
Obbink, Dirk. 2014a. "New Poems by Sappho." *Times Literary Supplement*. 5 February 2014. www.the-tls.co.uk/articles/public/new-poems-by-sappho/. (accessed 21 October 2021)

Obbink, Dirk. 2014b. "Two New Poems by Sappho." *ZPE* 189: 32–49.
Obbink, Dirk. 2015. "Provenance, Authenticity, and the Text of the New Sappho Papyri." Paper delivered at the 146th Annual SCS Meeting. January 2015. www.papyrology.ox.ac.uk/Fragments/SCS.Sappho.2015.Obbink.paper.pdf. (accessed 22 October 2021)
Obbink, Dirk. 2016a. "The Newest Sappho: Text, Apparatus Criticus, and Translation." In Bierl and Lardinois 2016, 13–33.
Obbink, Dirk. 2016b. "Ten Poems of Sappho: Provenance, Authenticity, and Text of the New Sappho Papyri." In Bierl and Lardinois 2016, 34–54.
O'Connell, Peter. 2018. "'Charaxus Arrived with a Full Ship!' The Poetics of Welcome in Sappho's Brothers Song and the Charaxus Song Cycle." *CA* 37: 236–266.
Page, Denys. 1955. *Sappho and Alcaeus: An Introduction to the Study of Ancient Lesbian Poetry*. Oxford: Oxford University Press.
Page, Denys. 1974. *Supplementum lyricis graecis: poetarum lyricorum graecorum fragmenta quae recens innotuerunt*. Oxford: Oxford University Press.
Parker, Holt. 1993. "Sappho Schoolmistress." *TAPA* 123: 309–351.
Parker, Holt. 2005. "Sappho's Public World." In Ellen Greene, ed., *Women Poets in Ancient Greece and Rome*, 3–24. Norman: University of Oklahoma Press.
Peponi, Anastasia-Erasmia. 2016. "Sappho and the Mythopoetics of the Domestic." In Bierl and Lardinois 2016, 225–237.
Pirenne-Delforge, Vinciane, and Gabriella Pironti. 2014. "Héra et Zeus à Lesbos: entre poésie lyrique et décret civique." *ZPE* 191: 27–31.
Raaflaub, Kurt. 2016. "The Newest Sappho and Archaic Greek-Near Eastern Interactions." In Bierl and Lardinois 2016, 127–147.
Rissman, Leah. 1983. *Love as War: Homeric Allusion in the Poetry of Sappho*. Königstein: Hain.
Rösler, Wolfgang. 1980. *Dichter und Gruppe: eine Untersuchung zu den Bedingungen und zur historischen Funktion früher griechischer Lyrik am Beispiel Alkaios*. München: W. Fink.
Romney, Jessica. 2019. "Group Identity and Archaic Lyric: We-group and Out-group in Alcaeus 129." In Peter Meineck, William Short, and Jennifer Devereaux, eds., *The Routledge Handbook of Classics and Cognitive Theory*, 191–201. London: Routledge.
Sabar, Ariel. 2020. "A Biblical Mystery at Oxford." *The Atlantic*. June 2020. https://www.theatlantic.com/magazine/archive/2020/06/museum-of-the-bible-obbink-gospel-of-mark/610576/. (accessed 22 October 2021)
Sampson, C. Michael. 2020. "Deconstructing the Provenances of P.Sapph.Obbink." *BASP* 57: 143–169.
Sampson, C. Michael, and Anna Uhlig. 2019. "The Murky Provenance of the Newest Sappho." *Eidolon*. 5 November 2019. https://eidolon.pub/the-murky-provenance-of-the-newest-sappho-aca671a6d52a. (accessed 22 October 2021)
Schlesier, Renate. 2013. "Atthis, Gyrinno, and Other Hetairai: Female Personal Names in Sappho's Poetry." *Philologus* 157: 199–222.
Skinner, Marilyn. 1993. "Woman and Language in Archaic Greece, or, Why is Sappho a Woman?" In Nancy Rabinowitz and Amy Richlin, eds., *Feminist Theory and the Classics: Thinking Gender*, 125–144. New York: Routledge
Skinner, Marilyn. 2014. *Sexuality in Greek and Roman Culture*. Second edition. Chichester: Wiley and Sons.
Snyder, Jane. 1997. *Lesbian Desire in the Lyrics of Sappho*. New York: Columbia University Press.
Stanley, Keith. 1976. "The Role of Aphrodite in Sappho Fr.1." *GRBS* 17: 305–321.
Stehle, Eva. 1981. "Sappho's Private World." *Women's Studies* 8: 47–63.

Stehle, Eva. 1990. "Sappho's Gaze: Fantasies of a Goddess and Young Man." *differences* 2: 88–125.
Stehle, Eva. 1997. *Performance and Gender in Ancient Greece: Nondramatic Poetry in Its Setting.* Princeton: Princeton University Press.
Stehle, Eva. 2016. "Larichos in the Brothers Poem: Sappho Speaks Truth to the Wine-Pourer." In Bierl and Lardinois 2016, 266–292.
Swift, Laura. 2018. "Thinking with Brothers in Sappho and Beyond." *Mouseion* 15: 71–87.
Trumpf, Jürgen. 1973. "Über das Trinken in der Poesie des Alkaios." *ZPE* 12: 139–160.
Tsomis, Georgios. 2001. *Zusammenschau der frühgriechischen monodischen Melik (Alkaios, Sappho, Anakreon).* Stuttgart: Franz Steiner.
Vidan, Aida. *Embroidered with Gold, Strung with Pearls: The Traditional Ballads of Bosnian Women.* Cambridge, MA: Harvard University Press.
Voigt, Eva-Maria. 1971. *Sappho et Alcaeus: Fragmenta.* Amsterdam: Polak and van Gennep.
West, Martin. 2014. "Nine Poems of Sappho." *ZPE* 191: 1–12.
Williamson, Margaret. 1995. *Sappho's Immortal Daughters.* Cambridge, MA: Harvard University Press.
Wilson, Lyn. 1996. *Sappho's Sweetbitter Song: Configurations of Female and Male in Ancient Greek Lyric.* London: Routledge.
Winkler, Jack. 1981. "Gardens of Nymphs: Public and Private in Sappho's Lyrics." *Women's Studies* 8: 65–91.
Yatromanolakis, Dimitrios. 2007. *Sappho in the Making: The Early Reception.* Washington, DC: Center for Hellenic Studies.
Yatromanolakis, Dimitrios. 2009. "Alcaeus and Sappho." In Felix Budelmann, ed., *The Cambridge Companion to Greek Lyric*, 204–226. Cambridge: Cambridge University Press.

Reframing Iphis and Caeneus: Trans Narratives and Socio-Linguistic Gendering in Ovid's *Metamorphoses*

J. L. WATSON

Abstract

This article argues for a reinterpretation of two Ovidian characters. Iphis (in Book 9 of the *Metamorphoses*) and Caeneus (in Book 12) have historically been described by a range of sexualities and gender terms, such as *lesbian*, *transvestite*, and *transsexual*, each of which comes with its own problems. Here, I reframe these characters as *trans* men. In this article I build on two strands of classical scholarship to develop a socio-linguistic framework in which Iphis and Caeneus may be seen as male. First, using previous work on Latin grammatical gender, I examine Iphis and the way that Ovid utilizes grammatical gender and semantic situation to cast him as somewhat male throughout the narrative. Second, I explore how the socially constructed model of Roman masculinity, in which to be masculine is to be a sexual penetrator, confers masculinity on Caeneus, even though Ovid does not provide an explicit scene in which he sexually penetrates someone else. By combining these two strands, I argue that Ovid's Iphis and Caeneus are presented linguistically and socially as male, although in different ways to each other. Such an approach has value in twenty-first-century academia by examining how Iphis and Caeneus have been used as touchstones for modern female homosexuality and how, in the future, they may also fulfil the same function for modern trans people.

The reality of gendered experience in the ancient world, even for those with normative gender identities, is notoriously difficult for modern scholarship to reconstruct. Such complexities are compounded when we are confronted by genders that exist outside of a standard cis binary.[1] The question of whether and how trans identities and performances may have operated during antiquity is even more elusive

---

1. The terms *cis* and *trans* are capacious and both terms are often suffixed by "-sexual" or "-gender"; for why I avoid these suffixes, see below. Broadly speaking, cis describes a gender identity, presentation, or performance that corresponds to the sex an individual was assigned at birth, whereas trans may describe gender identities, presentations, or performances that in some way differ from the sex assigned at birth. These designations exist at opposite ends of a spectrum, and there may be a large range of identities, presentations, and performances between them.

than it is for normative genders.² What is clear from the text of the *Metamorphoses* is that Ovid is questioning and problematizing the boundaries of gender and sexuality in his presentation of Iphis and Caeneus, whose gendered characterization may or may not reflect a reality of Augustan Rome. Ovid's exploration of gender and sexuality in these two narratives has been interpreted through a number of labels—lesbianism, transvestitism, and transsexuality—none of which fully map onto how Ovid casts Iphis and Caeneus (see Part I below). This article applies a label new to scholarship, *trans*, in order to explore how masculinity and maleness play out in the tales of Iphis in Book 9 and Caeneus in Book 12.³ These two men experience their maleness differently, and so I will deal with them differently. In Part II, my primary hermeneutic approaches to Iphis's gender will be the work of Anthony Corbeill (2015) on the relationships between Latin grammatical gender and 'biological' sex, and Enrico Giaccherini's (2005) theory of metamorphosis in which, though the exterior may change, there is always an "integrity of the self that remains."⁴ For Caeneus, in Part III, I focus on the discursive methods by which the Romans defined the category of 'man' and how they obtain in his narrative.

Here, then, I argue that Ovid, through the way he deploys language and the social model of penetrative masculinity from the beginnings until the ends of Iphis's and Caenus's tales, paints both characters as possessing a masculinity that reflects an ontological maleness. He does this both by manipulating the potential powers of gendering inherent to Latin grammar and by playing heavily on themes of penetration and its significance to Roman manhood, thereby creating a socio-linguistic framework in which the maleness of Iphis and Caeneus is foregrounded. In this article, I critically examine the value of trans-centric approaches to interpretations of Latin literature, asking two questions: "If we apply a modern category of gender to ancient literary figures, how does this impact our understanding of Roman gender?" And, "Why does it matter to conceive of Iphis, Caeneus, and other figures from the ancient world as being genders which are different from their birth sex?"

My choice of subjects for this paper is not random. Donald Lateiner (2009, 131) has estimated that there may be up to seven narratives in the *Metamorphoses* which fit under the broad umbrella 'trans' (for which, see below): Tiresias (3.316–350), Sithon (4.279–280), Hermaphroditus (4.274–388), Mestra (8.853–854), Iphis (9.666–797), Caeneus (12.169–209, 459–535), and the Coroni (13.697–699). Of these, only Iphis and Caeneus clearly live in their 'chosen' gender consistently and perma-

---

2. Even in mythology, trans characters are rare; see Forbes Irving 1990, 149–170.

3. The term *masculinity* refers to a mode of performance or gesture, undertaken by people of a range of genders, whereas *maleness* implies an ontological claim about what kind of gender someone is.

4. Giaccherini 2005, 62; see Corbeil 2015. *Contra* Begum-Lees 2020, who sees the continuity of this 'integrity of self' as evidence that Iphis's metamorphosis is unresolved.

nently after transition. In the case of the Coroni, it is unclear whether they are trans men formed from the ashes of Menippe and Metioche, or male 'children' born from the ashes. Iphis and Caeneus, therefore, represent a unique object of inquiry for this paper.[5]

I The Use of Trans Terminology for Iphis and Caeneus

I begin with two points relating to terminology. First, I use he/him/his pronouns for both Iphis and Caeneus to represent the end result of their stories, although where Ovid has explicitly used a feminine verbal form of Iphis or Caeneus, I translate it using she/her/hers. It is now standard in scholarship to refer to Iphis and Caeneus by she/her/hers pronouns,[6] a decision that may at least be questioned given the conclusion of their tales, and one I shall therefore aim to rectify. Second, I use 'trans' throughout this article for two reasons: first, as a productive anachronism to foreground trans-centered approaches and, second, as a broad, capacious designation that avoids determining such characters' genders too precisely and, therefore, exclusively. My use of trans also aims to consciously avoid perpetuating potentially harmful terms (such as transsexual), while still capturing the gender-crossing and sex-crossing dynamics at play in Ovid's poem.[7] A term like trans

---

5. Cf. examples of cross-dressing, in which there is no existential change, merely a different garb, such as Jupiter's rape of Callisto at *Met.* 2.422–438 or Vertumnus's seduction of Pomona at 14.643–660.

6. She/her/hers is used, exclusively or almost exclusively, by, inter alia, Anderson 1972, Hallett 1997, Wheeler 1997, Hill 1999, Raval 2002, Pintabone 2002, Walker 2006, Boehringer 2007 (in French and with agreeing feminine adjective terminations), Williams 2010, Kamen 2012. Ormand (2005) uses mostly she/her/hers but also he/him/his sporadically; Lateiner (2009, 136–139) insists on he/she (i.e., using both sets of pronouns in conjunction), while Maisel (2019) uses he/him/his throughout.

7. The literature on these trans narratives has yet to establish consistent terminology, but some scholars have employed confusing descriptions, such as Lateiner's (2009) use of "bisexual" to mean 'of duplex biological sex,' instead of the usual 'sexual attraction to two sexes/genders.' In such cases modern categories such as 'intersex' are perhaps clearer. Similarly, Carlà-Uhink (2017) oddly uses "transgender dynamics" to describe the phenomenon of people being denigrated by being described as being like the opposite biological sex, e.g., a manly woman or effeminate man. This is surely different from the sort of ontological statement normally meant by 'transgender.' Because of the nature of this paper's subject, scholarly work directly germane to my interpretation of Iphis and Caeneus as trans men has tended to appear in the new media of online journals, such as *Eidolon* (e.g., Barish 2018, Franklin 2018, Maisel 2019, Clarke 2019). *Productive anachronism* (δημιουργικός αναχρονισμός) is a term proposed by Papanikolaou 2014, 14, to describe the utility of deploying terms like *gay* or *queer* in the context of people who had no access to the terms themselves. Papanikolaou principally uses the term for the twentieth-century Greek poet, Constantine Cavafy.

may be seen to describe a too ipso facto modern category of gender; however, I argue, it can be useful in examining people from antiquity. Other terms common in the existing scholarly literature on such themes (transvestite, transsexual, etc.) are often inaccurate (that is, Caeneus is not merely cross-dressing, but exists in an ontological state of maleness) and may perpetuate harmful language often directed at modern trans people. The paradox of discussing characters who clearly fall under our concept of transgender, but for whom the Romans had no equivalent label, is neatly summed up by Roland Barthes in *S/Z* (1974, 190–191): "Even though the connotation may be clear, the nomination of its signified is uncertain, approximative, unstable: to fasten a name to this signified depends in large part on the critical pertinence to which we adhere."

The word transgender was first coined in 1965 by John F. Oliven (1968, 514).[8] Since the mid-1980s, its use has steadily become more widespread, and trans is now a common word in modern media. The label of transgender as we now understand it does not map neatly onto the axes of gender, presentation, and performance seen in the ancient world, but, as Filippo Carlà-Uhink (2011, 3) states in the introduction to *TransAntiquity*, "In Classical Antiquity, it is possible to identify forms of behaviour and action which might fall into our modern category of transgender."[9] Despite Carlà-Uhink's optimism, I use trans throughout this article, rather than transgender, so as to avoid making specific claims about Iphis's and Caeneus's identities (that is, how they, two literary characters, identified themselves) while preserving the terminology necessary to depict Ovid's presentation of them. When I combine trans with the word man (trans man), I am describing someone who is born biologically female but who becomes a man (whatever that means) through transition. H. Christian Blood (2019) has said of the label trans that it "privileges the diversity of gender identity and expression beyond a traditional continuum, which places the practice of cisgender female and male identity on one end, and gender confirmation surgery on the other," and reminds us that trans "experiences are varied, personal, and subtle."[10] It is this sort of comprehen-

---

8. Previous appellations had existed before Oliven, such as Hirschsfeld's (1923) coinage "Transsexualismus." Although Hirschfeld himself uses this term in much the way that modern society uses transgender, its English counterpart transsexual can be offensive and may privilege the voices of post-operational trans people in addition to centering surgery as the be-all-and-end-all of trans identities.

9. Cf. Clarke 2019 (square brackets indicate my edits): "Twenty-first century identities don't map onto easily [sic] ancient figures, nor should they. Conceiving of dead Greeks and Romans as 'gay[/trans]' is not useful, and it is likewise useless to depict them as 'straight[/cis].'"

10. Quotations from pp. 168 and 166, respectively. As Blood (185–186) notes, other similarly capacious terms have been used by trans theorists in the past (for instance, trans*), but these have been seen to privilege the voices and identities of post-transition binary trans folk (i.e., binary trans men and women).

sive and nonspecific approach to labelling which seems to make the most sense in the cases of Iphis and Caeneus, as, despite the similarities between their narratives, both men are trans in different ways.

As I outline in Part III, Caeneus's experience of gender resembles more closely the experience of those modern, binary trans men who transition socially and corporeally and live out the remainder of their lives as men, with few caveats to that experience. We see less of Caeneus's internal struggle than we do of Iphis's, so the narrative presents his transition as far more cut-and-dry. Iphis, however, faces a different trans experience. From the beginning of his life, he is socially gendered as a boy/man. Other than his mother and himself, everyone who interacts with him reads him as a man (or at least a *puer*). In contrast to Caeneus's simple, binary transition, Iphis faces an internal conflict between the way he is perceived by the world and the way he perceives himself, especially as he relates to his beloved, Ianthe. His transition is more fraught and seems almost a compromise: 'man' is the best fitting category for what he is in the social setting in which he exists. So, then, in the cases of Iphis and Caeneus, we see two individuals who are born female, as defined by anatomical sex, but who, for differing, though similarly sexual, reasons, employ divine intervention to 'transform' themselves into men, even if their masculinities are different from one another. This explains why Ovid employs different techniques to mark their transitions.

A brief summary of both narratives and the transitions they describe is in order before I analyze Ovid's depiction of Iphis's and Caeneus's genders in Parts II and III, respectively.

Caeneus, living then as a beautiful Thessalian Lapith named Caenis, was raped by Neptune and subsequently offered a reward in compensation from the god; he requested as his reward that he would never be penetrated again (12.201–203; more on this passage in Part III). Neptune understands this as a desire to be a fierce hero, and Caenis becomes Caeneus, the Lapith hero whom no blade can penetrate, and whose eventual death is only brought about by his being crushed by trees (I return later to this penetrative theme).

Iphis was born to a family unable to raise a daughter; thus, when he is born, his mother raises him as a boy and his oblivious father gives him the androgynous name Iphis. At the age of 13, Iphis is betrothed to a girl, Ianthe, but he fears that his secret birth sex will be discovered when they marry; thus, Iphis and his mother pray to the goddess Isis, who fully "transforms" him into a man (9.786–791):

> sequitur comes Iphis euntem,
> quam solita est, maiore gradu; nec candor in ore
> permanet, et vires augentur et acrior ipse est
> vultus et incomptis brevior mensura capillis,

plusque vigoris adest habuit quam femina. nam quae 790
femina nuper eras, puer es.

Iphis followed as a companion to his mother as she went, with a greater stride than she [Iphis] was used to; and no whiteness remained in his face, and his strength grew, and his very face was sharper, and his hairdo was shorter and unkempt, and there was more vigor in him than a woman has. For you who were recently a woman, are now a boy![11]

Ovid, importantly, shies away here from explicitly narrating the graphic reality of these metamorphoses; usually in his epic, he is unafraid of providing either a cinematic montage of transformed body parts,[12] or evocations of genitalia.[13] But with Caeneus and Iphis, he is content to tell us that the change has taken place almost exclusively through secondary characteristics, such as the deepening of Caeneus's voice and Iphis taking longer strides.[14] This is remarkable since the probable source for Ovid's Iphis—the story of Leucippus from Nicander's lost *Heteroeumena*[15] now preserved only in Antoninus Liberalis's later *Metamorphoses*—seems to have been graphic:[16] [οἱ Φαίστιοι] θύουσι Φυτίῃ Λητοῖ, ἥτις ἔφυσεν **μήδεα** τῇ κόρῃ ("[The people of Phaestum] sacrifice to Leto the Grower,[17] since she grew **male genitals** on a girl," 17).

---

11. All translations are my own.
12. E.g., Callisto's painfully slow transformation into a bear (*Met.* 2.476–485) or the extended, body-part-by-body-part description of the Maenads who murdered Orpheus metamorphosing into oaks (11.67–84).
13. E.g. *Met.* 4.359–367, where Salmacis's assault on Hermaphroditus is characterized in terms strongly evocative of genitalia, e.g., *serpens* ("snake," 362), *hederae* ("ivy," 365), *longos truncos* ("long trunks," 365), and *polypus* [...] / *ex omni dimissis parte flagellis* ("an octopus with its tentacles sent out from all over," 366–367); see Nagle 1984, 251–252. Cf. *Met.* 10.475: *pendenti nitidum vagina deripit ensem* ("He snatched his glistening 'sword/penis' from the hanging 'sheath/vagina'").
14. Ormand (2005, 99) sees these features as proof that the transformation is about the external performance of gender—biological sex seems unimportant to Ovid in this story. See Gleason 1995, 60–70, for the importance of traits like hair and gait as indicators of masculinity in the ancient world.
15. See Bömer 1977, 469–472. For the *Heteroeumena*, see *Brill's New Pauly*, s.v. "Nicander."
16. Wheeler (1997, 200) detects an allusion to this more physical metamorphosis with Iphis's increasing *vigor* at *Met.* 9.790.
17. On the shift from Leto to Isis, see Ormand 2005, 100. He emphasizes Isis's functionality as an "emblem for the ideology of gender" because of her husband Osiris's lack of penis (*Met.* 9.963: *numquam satis quaesitus Osiris* ["Osiris never fully found"]). I agree and submit as further evidence her phallic horns, which almost substitute Osiris's lack: *Met.* 9.688–689: *inerant lunaria fronti / cornua* ("The moon's horns were on her forehead"), and 783–784: *imitataque lunam /*

The lack of graphic genital transformation in Ovid preserves a sense of ambiguity about Iphis and Caeneus; the male gender by which they are recognized post-metamorphosis is explicitly not defined by genitalia, even though it seems at least likely that both men had penises, something on which I elaborate below.[18] This takes on additional significance in the case of Iphis, who is 13 years-old at the point of his transformation;[19] 13 years would have been a fairly young age for a Roman man to marry, but it does loosely coincide with male puberty, biological and social, and the attendant Roman cultural practices, such as the removal of the *bulla* and the donning of the *toga virilis*, both practices that seem not to have occurred at a specific age in a boy's life, but rather when he was deemed to be entering puberty.[20] Therefore, the age at which Iphis gains his distinctly male secondary sex characteristics coincides with a Roman boy's participation in the coming of age rites that characterized his transition from childhood to manhood.

The debate is ongoing as to whether the story of Iphis is one of masculinized lesbianism,[21] in which, to use Judith Hallett's words (1997), the Roman *milieu* denies female homoeroticism's "reality" and "corrects" it by means of Iphis's sex-change and the establishment of a stable heteroerotic union, or whether this is the story of a trans man (e.g., Maisel 2019). I am not seeking to dismiss the interpretations of Iphis and Caeneus as proto-lesbians, and I will return later to the question of reception and identification in Part IV, and to the importance of these Ovidian characters as foundational classical texts for lesbianism. The story of Iphis is amenable to these sorts of feminist and lesbian interpretations, in which he becomes a 'masculinized lesbian,' because of the romantic aspect at the core of his story and the fact that he is clearly attracted to women, or at least to one woman. Kirk Ormand makes such an argument. Although he argues that at the core of the tale of Iphis there is "not a question of sexuality but of gender,"[22] he does focus on the

---

cornua fulserunt ("Her horns, shaped like the moon, glowed"). For *cornua* as evoking typically male genitalia, see Adams 1990, 21–22.

18. There may be an oblique reference to Caeneus's male genitalia at *Met.* 12.486: *longaque amplectitur ilia dextra* ("[Latreus] reached around his *ilia* with his long right arm"). For the sexual connotations of *ile*, see below; for Iphis's genital evocation, also below.

19. For 13 years of age: *tertius interea decimo successerat annus* ("Meanwhile, 13 years had passed by," 9.714). Iphis occupies an exact midpoint between the lawful ages of consent to a marriage: 12 for girls and 14 for boys; see Rawson 1999, 21. However, it was unusual for Roman men to wed so young, and it appears that 25 may have been an average age; see Saller 1987, esp. 29, and Treggiari 1991, 39–43, 399–400.

20. For more on Roman coming of age rituals, see Dolansky 1997. For the concept of "social puberty," Harrill 2002, 255.

21. See, e.g., Ormand 2005, Walker 2006, Barish 2018, Franklin 2018.

22. Ormand 2005, 91–98 (quotation from 95).

physical similarities between Iphis and Ianthe,[23] rather than noting their differences. Despite his interpretation being largely focused on gender, the basis for Ormand's argument is that Iphis and Ianthe's relationship is characterized by (feminine) mutuality, rather than one party's masculine dominance. I argue that Ovid does present Iphis as a masculine, dominant character, as may be seen in his deployment of the key word *potior* and the punning word-order of the final line of Book 9: *potiturque sua puer Iphis Ianthe* (for which see below). Indeed, Ovid may say that Iphis and Ianthe shared an *aequum* [...] *vulnus* ("the same wound," 9.720–721), perhaps figuring that both parties, at this point in the narrative, have vaginas, but he crucially follows this up by saying that they had *fiducia dispar* ("different expectations," 9.721). Iphis and Ianthe are very much alike, but as I discuss below, they undergo different puberties, and Iphis, through divine intervention, grows into his maleness.

Caeneus, in whose narrative there is no sexual or romantic intrigue beyond his initial rape, is harder to reclaim as a masculinized lesbian, and so has received less overall focus in scholarship, both on gender and on the *Metamorphoses* generally. However, like Iphis, Caeneus can be (re)considered as a trans man, whose transness can be the focus of reclamatory scholarship. Unlike Iphis, whose ontological maleness is challenged by the internal strife of gender dysphoria (see below), Caeneus's gender is questioned by characters in the text (as I discuss in more detail in Part III). This questioning provides Ovid with an opportunity to explicitly vindicate what makes Caeneus a man: his military prowess and dominance, which acts as a stand-in for masculine sexual prowess. The practicality of a capacious term like trans, as opposed to transsexual, is precisely that Iphis's and Caeneus's genitalia are not relevant to their genders; even if he is anatomically like Ianthe, her perception—and the perception of the world at large—is that Iphis is a man; even if Latreus has heard rumors about Caeneus's purported feminine origin, he is proven fatally wrong in believing that this gossip is relevant to Caeneus on the battlefield.

II Iphis and Linguistic Gendering

I focus here on the use of grammatical gender, primarily in the tale of Iphis, although Ovid does employ some of the same techniques for Caeneus. In his *Sexing the World*, Anthony Corbeill (2005, 43–63) sets out the compelling argument that there is a strong relationship between Latin *genus* (grammatical gender) and *sexus* (biological sex), but with an allowance for fluctuation and change for specific

---

23. As stressed by Ovid at *Met.* 9.718–721; see also note 34 below.

reasons. He further asserts that nouns can change *genus* over time and that this must have impacted on the way that Romans viewed the biological or theoretical *sexus* of what the noun signified: "If a given noun, though not 'born a woman,' assumes a grammatically feminine gender, over time, this gender can facilitate the process by which the thing named accrues sexed qualities that speakers ultimately choose to identify as socially 'feminine'" (2015, 4), and "Personification—literally, 'person-making'—is a function of grammatical gender" (74).

The grammatical genders Ovid associates with Iphis (and Caeneus), therefore, cannot be inconsequential happenstance, and they impact powerfully on how we must read and interpret their metamorphoses. When examining the gendering of words Ovid uses for Iphis (and Caeneus), two things immediately become apparent: (1) there is relatively little gendering, whether through agreeing adjectives or substantives—for Iphis this creates a sense of ambiguity, and for Caeneus this is overwhelmingly masculinizing—and (2) in the case of Iphis, many words associated with him are in the neuter gender. I deal with these two points in sequence.

In the lengthy 131-line narrative of Iphis's birth and life, he is only gendered as masculine or feminine 23 times (15 feminine, eight masculine); Caeneus is gendered 39 times over 116 lines, with a majority (27) of these being masculinizing.[24] To focus on Iphis, then, Ovid seems to avoid using specifically gendered language of Iphis, preferring forms like non-periphrastic verbs and present participles that occlude the gender of their subject. The first explicit gendering, other than Iphis's name in line 668 (to which I will later return), is in line 705, where Ovid bluntly states, *nata est ignaro femina patre* ("She was born a girl to an unknowing father"). This is immediately undercut in the next line, where Iphis is described as semantically masculine: *iussit ali mater puerum mentita* ("The mother deceived and ordered that he be raised a boy"). Although there is no gendered pronoun for Iphis in this line, he is identified by the masculine noun *puer*. Lines 705 and 706 both have grammatically feminine subjects, though the person they denote has changed from Iphis to Telethusa, and in the second of the two lines, Iphis is no longer associated with the feminine words of that line, but is aligned with the masculine *puer*.

The few remaining uses of feminine grammatical gender occur mostly in Iphis's speech to himself; this section of the narrative accounts for almost half—seven out of 15—of the uses of the feminine gender of Iphis. In discussing this passage, I expound upon what hitherto has only been intimated: there is a conflict between

---

24. These statistics represent the number of clear statements of grammatical gender, not including proper nouns; thus, **nata est** ("she was born," 9.705) is counted as feminine instance, while *telaque in* **hunc** [...] *mittuntque* ("sent arrows at him," 12.495) is counted as a masculine instance.

Iphis's perception of his gender and the way he is gendered by the world around him. Iphis's gender is truly socially constructed, in that it is constructed by those who engage in gendered discourse with and about him, not least Ovid. We are told that *coniugium pactaeque exspectat tempora taedae, / quamque virum putat esse, virum fore credit Ianthe* ("Ianthe awaits her marriage and the day of her promised ceremony, and the woman she thinks to be a man, she believes will be her 'man,'" 9.722–723). Ovid artfully delays the name Ianthe to the end of the second line, which permits a possible initial reading where Iphis thinks of himself as a *vir*. From this, although Ovid shows us no such conversation, we can postulate that in conversation with or about Iphis, the people of Phaestum would have used *is/eum/eius* pronouns,[25] as he apparently passed for male enough for Ianthe to consider him a *vir*, playing on the double sense of this word as "man" and "husband."

The world at large genders Iphis as male but, in his aporetic speech (9.727–763), he repeatedly uses feminizing words of himself.[26] Indeed, the speech is bookended by two such instances, with one of its first words being *cognita* (9.727) and its last being *ambae* (9.763). Typically, this speech is presented as the principal evidence that Iphis is really a proto-lesbian, whose homoerotic desire for Ianthe is undercut by the impermissibility of same-sex female unions in ancient Rome.[27] However, L. K. M. Maisel (2019) argues that Iphis's

> despondency in anticipation of the wedding is not [...] about the incompatibility of 'her' same-sex desire and Ianthe's expectation of a male spouse, but instead (or at least with equal plausibility) comes out of his dysphoria about having a body sexed or gendered as female: 'what I want, ... she wants,' Iphis laments, 'but nature does not.'

Maisel alludes to lines 757–758: *quodque ego, vult genitor, vult ipsa, socerque futurus. / at non vult natura, potentior omnibus istis* ("And what I want, is what my father wants, what she wants, and what my father-in-law-to-be wants. But nature does not want it, more powerful than all of them"). Maisel's identification of this

---

25. At line 9.779, Telethusa uses a feminine form, *haec*, of Iphis, but given that she is the only other mortal in on the secret, this seems fitting.

26. *Cognita* (727), *nulla* (735), *virgine* (743), *ipsa* (745), *nata, ipsam* (747), and *ambae* (763). There is a debate around *nulla*, as to whether the wish *vellem nulla forem* is a desire not to be a woman (Anderson 1972, 470) or to die (Bömer 1977, 495; Hill 199, 163). I am sympathetic to the former; cf. *Met.* 12.202 of Caeneus: *da femina ne sim*.

27. See Hallett 1997; Pintabone 2002; Ormand 2005; Walker 2006; Lateiner 2009, 137–138; Kamen 2012; Oliven 2015, 285. Each provides a slightly different angle on 'proto-lesbianism' but none except Ormand deal with potential question of gender at any length.

scene with a form of gender dysphoria is intriguing and, I suggest, persuasive.[28] Iphis's whole speech is marked by a series of disconnects between his entire life up until this point and anxiety about what marrying Ianthe would mean for him and his gender; mostly, he is concerned with sex. Throughout the speech, Iphis's principal worry is *nec tamen [Ianthe] est potienda tibi* ("And yet [Ianthe] is never to be 'had' by you," 9.753). Iphis cannot distinguish between his desire for Ianthe and his body, the anatomy of which precludes normative, penetrative sex with his bride-to-be.[29] Indeed, the anxiety around penetration is his soliloquy's last thought. In the final line, *sacra, quibus qui ducat abest, ubi nubimus ambae* ("rites, from which the man who leads is missing, where we both as women marry," 9.763), Iphis plays on the parallel verbs of marriage: *ducere* for men, *nubere* for women.[30] Iphis fears a marriage from which the masculine principle (*qui ducat*) is absent, and the consequence of which is an unthinkable union between two women. Indeed, this constitutes the only use of the first-person plural form of *nubere* in extant Latin, underscoring how impossible a sentiment it was in the Roman context for two women to marry one another. As with his use of the verb *potior*, Iphis's fear about being one of two women getting married is dramatically ironic to the knowing reader, who is aware that Iphis will, in fact, play the part of *qui ducat* by the end of the tale.

This monologue, then, is littered with Iphis's self-description with feminizing words. Would this not be a clear argument that he self-identifies as a woman with Sapphic desires? Such an interpretation may underplay the fraught emotions of the speech. Iphis's self-alignment with femininity is concurrent with his self-alignment with monstrosity. He contrasts his predicament with a *naturale malum saltem* ("normal, natural evil," 9.730) and likens himself to the *monstrum* ("monstrosity," 9.735) of Pasiphaë's zoophilic lust for the Cretan bull, claiming that his case is *furiosior* ("more frenzied," 9.737) because of his gender troubles. Iphis's self-hatred at a moment of extreme gender dysphoria comes as no surprise to readers familiar

---

28. Gender dysphoria is defined by the American Psychiatric Association 2013, 451, as "the distress that may accompany the incongruence between one's experienced or expressed gender and one's assigned gender." I do not propose to retroactively diagnose a mythical, literary creation with a modern medical category, simply to indicate that there are experiential parallels. Lateiner (2009, 138) also uses the term *gender dysphoria* of Iphis but only in passing and without a critical examination of what is usually meant by this term with relation to trans people.

29. Kamen (2012, 22) argues that non-penetrative sex, such as that which would have happened between Iphis and Ianthe without a genital metamorphosis, was uniquely unnatural to the Romans.

30. For the gendered uses of these verbs, see Treggiari 1991, 166–167 (for *ducere*) and 164 (for *nubere*).

with the dysmorphic aspects of gender dysphoria that some trans people experience. This sort of self-hatred and obsession with the mismatch between how everyone perceives Iphis (as a boy) and how his anatomy is (inept for penetrative sex) characteristic of the modern medical diagnostic tools used to identify gender dysphoria in trans people. The fifth edition of the *Diagnostic and Statistical Manual of Mental Disorders* (hereafter, *DSM-V*) states that some young trans men "may express a desire to have a penis or claim to have a penis or that they will grow one when they are older" (453). Iphis makes no claim to possess a penis, but he does express a desire to be a boy: *num [Daedalus] me puerum de virgine doctis / artibus efficiet?* ("Surely [Daedalus] would not make me a boy from a girl with his learned techniques?," 9.743–744). Iphis may consider the transformation an impossibility (as evinced by his use of *num*), but he is diegetically unaware that he is a creation within Ovid's *Metamorphoses*, a poem predicated on impossible transformations, and so readers should be alert to Ovid's suggestion that some great craftsman, an expert in *artes*, can achieve just this bodily adjustment. It cannot be denied, then, that Ovid uses grammatically feminizing words of Iphis, but we should not ignore the context in which many of them appear, within a speech full of self-loathing.

We now turn to the use of the neuter gender and ambiguous gendering in the tale of Iphis. It is important to note that the neuter grammatical gender does not equate to something approaching modern non-binary people,[31] and it cannot be used of living creatures. It is usually treated as separate from the polarity of masculine versus feminine by scholars of Latin grammar, both ancient and modern:

> vel principalia vel sola genera duo sunt, masculinum et feminum. (Donatus, *Gramm. mai.* 4.375.20 Keil)[32]
> There are two grammatical genders—masculine and feminine—either principally or exclusively.

> nullam rem animalem neutro genere declinari. (Varro, fr. 8 Kent)
> No living thing is to be inflected by the neuter gender.

---

31. The term *non-binary* describes individuals who do not identify with either binary maleness or binary femaleness. It is a capacious term that may describe a range of gender identities, performances, and presentations. Note: many modern non-binary people, when using neo-Latin, do not choose to refer to themselves with the neuter grammatical gender, due to its dehumanizing effect. See, e.g., Lupercal's guide for gender inclusivity in the Latin language: https://web.archive.org/web/20210226160631/https://www.lupercallegit.org/post/a-style-guide-for-gender-inclusivity-in-the-latin-language (accessed 1 November 2021).

32. Cf. Priscian, *Inst.* 5.1.

genera dicta a generando. quicquid enim gignit aut gignitur, hoc potest genus dici et genus facere. (Varro, fr. 7a Kent)

Grammatical genders are named from the act of generation. For whatever gives birth or is born, that can be called a *genus* and can make a *genus*.

Despite the general reluctance to ascribe cultural significance to a word being neuter in gender, Corbeill (2015, 6) does admit that

The types of words that tend to be marked with this gender include those describing classes or collections of objects and ideas (such as the neuter noun *genus* itself), those with functions perceived as passive (the internal organs), *or those that are the product of becoming* (e.g., neuter fruits are normally conceived as the products of feminine trees). (my emphases)

It may, therefore, be significant that Iphis, whose narrative in the *Metamorphoses* is concerned with his becoming—in self-perception and perhaps biology—what most of the world already perceives him to be, is characterized with the neuter, a grammatical gender that denotes a process of becoming. In his narrative, Iphis is described using neuter language while *in utero* (*pondus*, 9.685, 704), which is not atypical of how Latin authors conceived of fetuses.[33] As Corbeill would say, fetuses "are the product of becoming." However, the goddess Isis demands that his mother *nec dubita* [...] / *tollere quicquid erit* ("Do not hesitate to raise it, whatever [gender] it will be," 9.698-699). Although Iphis is, at this point in the narrative, within his mother's womb and so a neuter word (*quicquid*) may be expected, Isis's use of the future tense (*erit*) forces a reader to imagine the future child after birth and to imagine him as a neuter noun. This creates a sense of potentiality for the child—its gender is as yet undetermined, as it exists in a neuter state of becoming, even once born. This ambiguity of gender is preserved in Iphis's physical appearance: *facies, quam sive puellae, / sive dares puero, fuerat formosus uterque* ("His face would be equally beautiful if you gave it to a girl or a boy," 9.712-713).[34] The potentiality of Iphis's gender is left open by his name.

The name Iphis merits further attention. Ovid states that the name Iphis "was of common gender" (*commune foret*, 9.710), but the gender of the Latin proper

---

33. Unborn children are often neuter in Latin; see, e.g., Lucretius 4.1250; Propertius 4.1.100; Ovid, *Am.* 2.13.1, 2.13.20, 2.14.14, *Her.* 4.58, 6.120, 11.37, 11.38, 11.42, *Met.* 10.481; Phaedrus 1.18.5; [Quintilian], *Decl.* 6.10, 8.13; Pliny, *HN* 7.41; Statius, *Theb.* 2.615, 7.166, *Silv.* 3.4.77. For *pondus* indicating an unborn child, see *TLL* 10.1.2618.21-38, s.v. "pondus."

34. Ormand (2005, 99) sees this "genderlessness" as a constitutive part of being a *puer*. Pintabone (2002, 257) considers this description as evidence that Iphis is a manly woman, not a man in truth.

noun is unclear. In Greek, there are two separate names "Iphis,"[35] which look alike only in the nominative:[36]

	Feminine	Masculine
Nom.	ἡ Ἶφις	ὁ Ἶφις
Gen.	τῆς Ἴφιδος	τοῦ Ἴφιος
Dat.	τῇ Ἴφιδι	τῷ Ἴφι
Acc.	τὴν Ἴφιδα	τὸν Ἶφιν
Voc.	Ἶφις	Ἶφι

If, as Ovid claims, *Iphis* is of common gender in Latin,[37] then it declines as a mixture of the two Greek names, sometimes appearing feminine, and sometimes masculine:

	Common Gender	Greek Equivalent
Nom.	Iphis	ὁ/ἡ Ἶφις
Gen.	[Iphis/Iphidis]*	
Dat.	Iphidi/Iphi**	τῇ Ἴφιδι/ τῷ Ἴφι
Acc.	Iphin***	τὸν Ἶφιν
Abl.	Iphide	τῇ Ἴφιδι
Voc.	Iphi	Ἶφι

*There is no extant example of the Latin genitive.
**Both datives are attested in the epigraphic record, although *Iphi* only once at *CIL* 6.7288.[38]
***The accusative *Iphin* is not used of our Iphis, but of the Cypriot Iphis in *Met.* 14.

---

35. The masculine is attested at Euripides, *Supp.* 986, 1032, 1034; [Apollodorus], 3.63.9, 3.79.7 (father of Eteocles and Euadne), 3.60.4 (son of Alector); the feminine, at Homer, *Il.* 9.667; Philostratus, *Her.* 33.43 (Patroclus's beloved); [Apollodorus], 2.163.2 (Celeustanor's mother). Confusingly, the apparently feminine form Ἴφιδος is used in instances where it clearly refers to the father of Eteocles; see Aelian, *NA* 1.15.21, 6.25.1, the latter even accompanied by a masculine definite article (οἱ ποιηταὶ μὲν τὴν παῖδα τὴν **τοῦ Ἴφιδος** σέβουσι ["The poets honor the daughter of Iphis"). As Aelian is later than Ovid, perhaps he is drawing on the latter's use of a common gender name. Both forms of the name are fairly common in the Greek epigraphic record.

36. This word appears to have the sort of gender which Priscian (*Inst.* 5.2–3) would later call *mobile genus*. This term describes nouns that can happily be one or more genders, such as *filius/filia* or *natus/nata*. Priscian even explicitly lists certain names that "are [...] as if fluid, when feminine nouns are born from themselves, not from masculine nouns" (*sunt* [...] *quasi mobilia, cum a se, non a masculinis feminina nascuntur*, 5.3) such as Helenus and Helena.

37. *Lewis and Short Latin Dictionary* reconstructs two Latin names (one masculine, one feminine), Latinizing the Greek; however, Ovid's argument that it was a *nomen commune* implies that *Iphis* is a synthesis of the Greek words. There could, of course, be both a masculine and a feminine word in Latin, as *Lewis and Short* implies, but if so, Ovid uses the masculine of Iphis as well as the feminine; see below.

38. The date of this inscription is only slightly after Ovid, estimated at c. 31–56 CE.

The Latin name is rare outside of this particular myth[39] and refers to both men and women, as Ovid suggests.[40] The first encounter with Iphis's name in Book 9 is indisputably feminine, as it is paired with a participle in the feminine (*Iphide mutata* ["transformed Iphis," 9.668]), but subsequent uses are less clear. In line 709, it is used to name Iphis's grandfather, also called Iphis, so it designates a male signified and, as Stephen Wheeler (1997, 197) reminds us, giving our Iphis a *nomen avitum* "marks the child's masculine, patrilineal identity." In line 715, Ovid addresses Iphis in apostrophe, invoking the unexpected masculinizing vocative of *Iphi*, stemming from the Greek masculine vocative. Subsequently, every instance of the name in Book 9 is either in the vocative or the nominative, entirely occluding the feminizing aspects of the name's declension. The word *Iphi* is used long before the divinely appointed metamorphosis, and is in Ovid's authorial narration, not in a character's speech, which in some sense casts Iphis as masculine from his childhood.

Other aspects of the onomastics of Iphis point to his masculinity. Wheeler detects an etymological play in the relationship between Iphis's name and the Greek word ἶφι ("by force"), the instrumental from ἴς ("force").[41] He further points out the regular poetic etymologizing of ἴς with the Latin *vis* ("force"),[42] and thence to *vir* ("man").[43] Given that the original version of the Iphis story features a man called Leucippus, it is significant that Ovid has chosen to change the name to one with a specifically masculinizing force.

Ovid also exploits in the tale of Caeneus the relationship between grammatical *genus* and a character's gender. Caeneus is repeatedly gendered as male by Nestor, the narrator of his biography. Unlike Iphis, who *nata est* [...] *femina* ("was born [...] a woman," 9.705), Caeneus *femina natus erat* ("was born a woman," 12.175),[44]

---

39. In literary sources, Iphis is used only of men: Ovid, *Met.* 14.699, 717; Statius, *Theb.* 8.445, 447; Valerius, *Argon.* 1.441, 7.423. In the epigraphic record, the name is used of both men and women: men, *CIL* 6.7288; unclear gender, *CIL* 6.6334, 5.3636; women, *CIL* 6.9879, 6.19402, 6.23624, 6.23988, 9.6317, *AE* 1985 354.

40. The epigraphic record (above) does not attest a clearly 'masculinizing' case (i.e., vocative or accusative) being used of a woman, or vice versa.

41. Cf. the similar etymologizing onomastics in Iphigenia: ἶφι + γίγνομαι ("by force" + "I become").

42. Ernoult 1957, 117–18, 137–39.

43. Isidore, *Etym.* 11.2.17: *vir nuncupatus, quia maior in eo vis est quam in feminis: unde et virtus nomen accepit; sive quod vi agat feminam* ("Man is so-called because in him there is greater force than in women: from that 'strength' received its name: or else because he deals with a woman by force"). See also Ahl 1995, 156.

44. Cf. at Ovid, *Met.* 14.658–659, the example of Vertumnus, who is disguised as a woman but gives kisses *qualia numquam / vera dedisset anus* ("the sort that a real old woman never would have given"). Corbeill (2015, 99–100) argues that, although grammatically correct, the differing feminine terminations of *vera* and *anus* capture the dual-gendering of Vertumnus. See also Blood's

in a grammatically awkward synthesis of masculine participle (*natus*) and feminine complement (*femina*); this is simply the first of a series of masculinizing words used of the Lapith. Caeneus is feminized in two episodes of his overall narrative. The first is when we read of his birth and youth, when he was desired by eligible suitors of Thessaly and raped by Neptune.[45] This part of Caeneus's life is distanced from both Nestor's metadiegetic account of the war between the Centaurs and the Lapiths, and from the diegetic setting of the Achaean heroes swapping stories on the Trojan plain, when Nestor draws attention to the fact it is only a rumor (12.196–197, 200):

> secretaque litora carpens
> aequorei vim passa dei est (ita fama ferebat)
> ....
> (eadem hoc quoque fama ferebat).

Caeneus, as he was strolling along a lonely beach, suffered the power of the god of the sea (so the rumor goes) [...] (the same rumor also reports this).

Ovid apparently was the first person to tell the "rumor" of Caeneus's birth sex,[46] and so his first readership would be as surprised by the backstory as Nestor's Achaean audience. By cloaking the story as the rumor reported by a man, himself telling an entertaining fireside story of days gone by, Ovid effectively casts doubt on Caeneus's purported feminine origin and therefore affirms his masculinity. Narratologically, this reference to Caeneus's pre-transition youth comes crucially after Nestor has already established him as a male and masculine warrior, using appropriately masculine grammatical gendering (12.171–174):

> at ipse olim patientem vulnera mille
> corpore non laeso Perrhaebum Caenea vidi,
> Caenea Perrhaebum, qui factis inclitus Othryn
> incoluit, quoque id mirum magis esset in illo [...]

(2019, 164) discussion of the different grammatical genders at play in Apuleius, *Met.* 8.26: *sed puellae chorus erat cinaedorum.*

45. It is important to note that the exact moment when Caeneus is grammatically feminized (*passa*, 12.197) is through a verb (*patior*) which signals sexual passivity, often aligned with the feminine; see Adams 1990, 189–190, and Williams 2010, 157. See below for my comments on activity and passivity.

46. The story appears at Σ Apollonius of Rhodes 57–64a; the scholium is not precisely datable, but as Apollonius does not mention the gender-change himself, it is plausible that a much later scholiast is following Ovid, though he is not referenced.

But, I once saw Thessalian Caeneus himself, taking a thousand hits without his body being wounded, Thessalian Caeneus, who lived on Mt. Othrys, well known for his deeds, and also, what is even more miraculous about him [...]

A reader's first interaction with Caeneus, both in Ovid's *Metamorphoses*, and elsewhere in mythology, if they are familiar with his appearance in Argonautic myth (see below), is as a powerful male warrior. The rumor of feminine youth is framed as something distant and irrelevant to Caeneus's adult military and masculine prowess, as a deviation from the "integrity of the self that remains" (Giaccherini 2005, 62), which, as our twin narrators (Nestor and Ovid) assure us, presents no impediment to Caeneus's maleness.

The second instance of grammatically feminine words being used of Caeneus is during his one-on-one fight with the Centaur Latreus. Latreus snidely says that he cannot consider Caeneus a man because of how he was born and suggests that he partake in the feminine pursuit of weaving (12.475).[47] The battlefield taunt that one's foe is a woman was established in classical literature (e.g., Homer, *Il.* 2.235; Virgil, *Aen.* 9.617), but Ovid here develops this trope, teasing it out to its full ironic potential by having Latreus use it against Caeneus, who will shortly prove how inaccurate—and dangerous—it is to misgender him. Caeneus's response to being misgendered is to kill Latreus violently with two acts of penetration, first a spear throw, and then multiple stab wounds (12.470–478, 491–493). Through layering the diegesis (Ovid relates Nestor relating Latreus's speech), Ovid and Nestor each distance themselves from the feminizing words, making them part of someone else's speech, while Caeneus's gender is vindicated by his martial, penetrative victory over Latreus.

In the stories of both Iphis and Caeneus, then, grammatical gendering is used to reinforce their masculinity. Though Ovid does not exclusively use male gendering for the two characters, he is careful to undercut any feminizing words, either through immediate use of a counterbalancing masculine, or through distancing and challenging the discourse that seeks to feminize these men. The grammatical masculinity of these two men creates a textual reality in which Ovid recognizes an "integrity of the self" (Giaccherini 2005, 62), a male ontology whose proleptic encoding into grammatical structure allows a smooth transition into external masculine appearance.

---

47. Cf. Hector to Andromache at Homer, *Il.* 6.490–492: ἀλλ' εἰς οἶκον ἰοῦσα τὰ σ' αὐτῆς ἔργα κόμιζε, / ἱστόν τε ἠλακάτην τ', καὶ ἀμφιπόλοισι κέλευε / ἔργον ἐποίχεσθαι ("But having entered the house, attend to your own work, the loom and the distaff, and command your handmaidens to carry out their work"); see Freas 2018, 73.

III Caeneus and Social Gendering

The second major string to my argument focuses on what precisely the ontological state of being a *vir* ("man") meant to the Romans, and how this can be used to discuss the *vir*-ility of Iphis and, especially, Caeneus. Jonathan Walters (1993, 1997) has convincingly established that the gender role of the Roman *vir* was not fully synonymous with the biologically male sex, but was defined simultaneously by a peculiar state of impenetrability and the social expectation to sexually penetrate. Since this is most clearly articulated in the story of Caeneus, I shall deal with him in the first instance (12.201–203):

'magnum' Caenis ait 'facit haec iniuria votum,
tale pati iam posse nihil. da femina ne sim:
omnia praestiteris.'

Caenis said, "This injury gives me a great desire: no longer to be able to suffer like this; grant that I may not be a woman, and you will have given me everything.

Caeneus's metamorphosis, stemming from his penetrative rape at the hands of Neptune, renders him impenetrable, both as a soldier whom no sword can pierce,[48] and as a *vir* whom no other man can sexually use. The language of Caeneus's rape is gendered. In Caeneus's wish above, as well as in Nestor's narration of the rape, a form of *patior* is used. In Nestor's description, the collocation *vim passa* figures the male aggressor as *vis*, an archetypally masculine notion (see above), set against the grammatically and notionally feminine *passa*.[49] The verb *patior* is associated with sexual and social submission, especially with the submission of women;[50] for example, Seneca the Younger claimed that women are "born to submit" (*pati natae*, *Ep.* 95.21). Therefore, Caeneus's wish "no longer to be able to suffer like this" (*tale pati iam posse nihil*) is essentially a duplicate of his other claim, *da femina ne sim* ("Grant that I may not be a woman"). Caeneus's desire is to leave behind the femi-

---

48. *Met.* 12.206–207: *nec saucius ullis / vulneribus fieri ferrove occumbere posset* ("And he could not become harmed by any wounds or die by the sword").

49. The phrase *vim patior* as a euphemism for rape, especially divine rape, is common in the *Metamorphoses*: 4.223 (Leucothoë's rape by Sol), 9.332 (Dryope's rape by Apollo), 11.309 (Chione's rape by Mercury).

50. See, e.g., Ovid, *Fast.* 2.178, 5.156; *Digesta* (Labeo) 36.2.30; Seneca, *Ep.* 95.21; Statius, *Theb.* 1.575. See also the use of the phrase *muliebra pati* and the discussion of it at Williams 2010, 157. *Patior* is sometimes used of a man's sexual submission, but only when the author is making a derogatory point about the man's lack of virility, e.g., Seneca, *QNat.* 16.2, *Prov.* 3.13.

nine realm of the semantics of *patior* and to gain access to the privileged world of sexual penetration, where he may cause *patientia* in others.

We can assess the significance of Ovid's use of the penetration theme by examining Caeneus in earlier literature. Although the first reference to Caeneus is at *Iliad* 1.264, the account of his impenetrability does not seem to predate an unclear reference in Pindar (fr. 167b Sandys): ὁ δὲ χλωραῖς ἐλάταισι τυπεὶς / ᾤχεθ᾽ ὑπὸ χθόνα Καινεὺς σχίσαις ὀρθῷ ποδὶ γᾶν ("But Caeneus, struck by the green fir-trees, went beneath the earth, having split the ground with his straight foot").

The account is more clearly laid out in Apollonius of Rhodes's *Argonautica* (1.59-64):

καινέα γὰρ ζῶόν περ ἔτι κλείουσιν ἀοιδοὶ
Κενταύροισιν ὀλέσθαι, ὅτε σφέας οἷος ἀπ᾽ ἄλλων   60
ἤλασ᾽ ἀριστήων· οἱ δ᾽ ἔμπαλιν ὁρμηθέντες
οὔτε μιν **ἐγκλῖναι** προτέρω σθένον, οὔτε **δαΐξαι**·
ἀλλ᾽ **ἄρρηκτος ἄκαμπτος** ἐδύσετο νειόθι γαίης,
θεινόμενος στιβαρῇσι καταΐγδην ἐλάτῃσιν.

For the bards tell that Caeneus, while living, perished at the hands of the Centaurs, when he drove through them, separate from the other heroes; the Centaurs, rushing back on him, **could neither first bend him, nor then split [his skin]**. But **unbroken** and **unbent**, he sank beneath the ground, being crushed by the avalanche of sturdy pines.

As elsewhere, Ovid takes a theme from his sources and provides it with an etiology.[51] Caeneus may always have been impervious to harm, but Ovid ties this into the specifically Roman conception of the impenetrable *vir*. The act of penetration he suffered as a youth results in him never being able to suffer again "this injustice" (*haec iniuria*, *Met*. 12.201) and renders him *imperfossus* ("impenetrable," 12.496).[52] Immediately after the metamorphosis, Ovid tells us that Caeneus "left, happy with his gifts, and lived out his days with manly pastimes [...] and

---

51. See Anderson 1996, 14–19. Cf., e.g., the owl accompanying Athena, unnamed in sources prior to Ovid, but given a name (Nyctimene) and full backstory at *Met*. 2.589–595 (cf. Hyginus, *Fab*. 204).

52. *Imperfossus* comes from *perfodio* ("dig through"); digging is a fairly common Latin metaphor for sex, for which Adams 1990, 151–152. The aural echo of *fossa* ("ditch"), which was an appellation for sexual orifices on both men and women (Adams 1990, 85–86, 113), should not be ignored. As the word *imperfossus* is probably an Ovidian coinage (Hill 1999, 215), it may have been created with such connotations in mind. This interpretation is *contra* Freas 2018, 61, who suggests that Caeneus does here succumb to the phallic onslaught of pine trees.

wandered the Thessalian fields" (*munere laetus abit studiisque virilibus aevum / exigit* [...] *Peneiaque arva pererrat*, 12.208–209). What precisely these *studia virilia* consisted of is unclear, but it is not implausible that Ovid is referring to Caeneus's newly penetrative sexual exploits.[53] *Arvum* can be a double-entendre for the vagina (see Adams 1990, 84) and in this context of practicing *studia virilia*, it does not seem implausible that Ovid is referring to Caeneus's penetration of Thessalian women. In addition, even if Ovid is not explicitly using *arva* here to refer to genitalia, Roman readers of the *Metamorphoses* would be alert to the fact that *arva* are frequently the site of sex and rape in the poem, for example, Io (1.597–600) and Europa (2.833–875).

Impenetrable Caeneus's role as penetrator is made clearer in his martial prowess, as Ovid-via-Nestor exploits the common Latin trope of war and fighting as metaphors for sex.[54] Caeneus's battle with Latreus plays out like a violent sex scene, in which Caeneus is the indisputable dominant partner (12.470–478, 491–493):

> 'et te, Caeni, feram? nam tu mihi femina semper,   470
> tu mihi Caenis eris. nec te natalis origo
> commonuit, mentemque subit, quo praemia facto
> quaque viri falsam speciem mercede pararis?
> quid sis nata vide, vel quid sis passa, columque,
> i, cape cum calathis et stamina pollice torque;   475
> bella relinque viris.' iactanti talia Caeneus
> extentum cursu missa latus eruit hasta,
> qua vir equo commissus erat.
> . . . .
>   capuloque tenus demisit in armos
> ensem fatiferum caecamque in viscera movit
> versavitque manum vulnusque in vulnere fecit.

"And do I have to put up with you, Caenis? For you will always be a woman to me, always 'Caenis' to me. Doesn't your birth sex remind you, doesn't it slip into your mind, the act for which you were rewarded, and by which reward you put on this false costume of a man? See what you were born as, or what you underwent, and go, take up a distaff and basket and spin the threads under your thumb." Caeneus threw his spear at the person saying these things, a spear sent to split open Latreus's side, stretched out midgallop, where the man was joined to the horse. [...] And Caeneus sunk his

---

53. See Freas 2018, 71; cf. Ziogas 2013, 200.
54. See Adams 1990, 157–159; also Preston 1916, 50, and Spies 1930, 51–53.

death-dealing sword up to the hilt in Latreus's side, unseen in his guts, and twisted and turned his hand, and made wound upon wound.

Caeneus begins the battle by swiftly killing five Centaurs (12.459–461), before facing up against Latreus; the Lapith's defeat of Latreus is liberally coded with metaphors for sexual penetration. First, he pierces the Centaur's side with his phallic spear (477),[55] then Latreus twice fails to pierce Caeneus's side (482, 485–486), and the second attempt actually destroys the Centaur's own phallic symbol, his sword.[56] Ovid barely keeps the sexual imagery subtextual here, having Latreus embrace Caeneus's *ilia* with his right hand (*longaque amplectitur ilia dextra*, 486).[57] *Ile* is an unusual choice of vocabulary, and clearly refers here to the lower midriff, but the *Thesaurus Linguae Latinae* also defines it as a technical term for the *arteriae a testiculis ad penem tendentes* ("arteries leading from the testicles to the penis").[58] The image becomes, then, one in which Latreus is masturbating Caeneus's superior penis, vindicating the latter's masculinity and, in turn, effeminizing himself, since stimulating a man's penis was considered a feminine sexual function.[59]

The most significant image in this scene is Caeneus's killing blows. Having figuratively emasculated his foe, he repeatedly stabs him (12.491–493). The dramatic image of Caeneus's multiple penetrations is unmistakable as synecdoche for the act of a Roman *vir* penetrating a passive male or female, with the polyptoton of *vulnusque in vulnere* ("wound upon wound") unsubtly configuring the orifice of such a person.[60] Caeneus, then, is not only a man and a *vir*, but a sort of

---

55. For *hastae* ("spears") as phallic, see Adams 1990, 19–20; that it strikes Latreus's *latus* ("side") may be significant, as *latus* can signify the site of sexual activity (Adams 1990, 49, 90).

56. Met. 12.488: *fractaque dissiluit percusso lammina callo* ("And the blade fell still, shattered upon striking the hard skin").

57. There often seems to be a contrast between the covert masturbatory left hand (e.g., Martial 9.41.1–2, 11.73; Lucilius 8.307) and the publicly martial or political right hand (e.g., Sallust, *Cat.* 58.8; Livy 1.1.8; Ovid, *Ars am.* 2.736). Cf. the rare usage of *dextra* as an agent of masturbation at Martial 11.29.1–2; it is there used similarly to our passage, of an external party pleasuring someone else's penis.

58. TLL 7.1.325.48, s.v. "ile." Catullus clearly uses *ile* to mean male genitalia at 11.20, 80.7–8 (cf. 63.5). The latter is Mynors's (1958) reading and describes Attis's self-castration; this seems to me to be proof enough to question Adams's (1990, 50–51) insistence that *ile* is only sexual as a metaphorical extrapolation from its primary meaning of "side."

59. See, e.g., Martial's poetry, where women frequently masturbate men in an attempt to arouse them: 6.23, 7.58, 10.55, 11.29. Martial 9.41 utilizes similar imagery, calling a man's masturbatory hand his *amica* ("girlfriend") and *paelex* ("mistress").

60. For *vulnus* as an orifice used sexually, see Adams 1990, 152. In his description of the blossoming love between Iphis and Ianthe, Ovid claims that *amor* ("love") gave both parties an *aequum vulnus* ("equal wound," 9.720–721), again preserving at least some ambiguity with regard to Iphis's gender. However, his subsequent comment that *erat fiducia dispar* ("It was an unequal pledge,"

'superman,' more powerfully penetrative than the other men he fights;⁶¹ his masculinity is not just vindicated, but supremely so. In addition, Caeneus's foes are not human men, but Centaurs, a race known for their sexual ferocity (Lawrence 1994, 59). Caeneus overcomes a masculine power itself more grotesquely extreme than normal human men. Nestor leaves no room for doubt in his Achaean audience as to Caeneus's masculinity.

This penetrative theme similarly exists in the narrative of Iphis's transition. The conclusion of Iphis's story, and indeed of Book 9, is precisely one of penetration. The last mention of Iphis has him sexually claiming his bride on their wedding night: *potiturque sua puer Iphis Ianthe* ("The boy Iphis 'had' his Ianthe," 9.797). *Potior* is a regular verb for a man's sexual conquest of a woman in Ovid (e.g., *Met.* 11.265), and even hints at male orgasm (Adams 1990, 188). The verb also reminds readers of Iphis's self-deprecating, and now manifestly false, comment in his soliloquy at line 753 that Ianthe "is not to be 'had' by you" (*nec* [...] *potienda tibi*). In a typically Ovidian play, the poet has placed *puer Iphis* physically in the line within *sua* [...] *Ianthe* (Raval 2002, 166–167), re-creating the act of penetration as the books' final image.⁶²

IV The Role of Trans-Centric Approaches in Twenty-First-Century Academia

I have argued that Iphis and Caeneus are in the language of modern English—even if this is not a language to which either they or Ovid had access—trans men. It is appropriate now to append a brief discussion of why such arguments are important and so rarely put forward by scholars. Historically, queer people have sought companionship in figures from the classical past in whom they recognize some aspect of themselves, normally an attraction to people of the same sex or gender.⁶³ For

---

9.721) implies that the futures for the lovers' "equal wounds" will be diverse, perhaps hinting at Iphis's eventual genital transformation, for which see below.

61. Lateiner 2009, 139, with Forbes-Irving 1990, 162.

62. There may also be a double-entendre in the votive plaque Iphis erects to Isis at *Met.* 9.797: DONA • PUER • SOLVIT • QUAE • FEMINA • VOVERAT • IPHIS ("Iphis the boy gives those 'gifts,' which he had promised as a woman"). Gifts as metonyms for marriage and/or sex are not uncommon in Greek: Theognis 2.1293–1294, and Plutarch, *Moralia* 777D. This is often combined with the gifts of the Muses, as at Athenaeus 11.8.4 and Anacreon, fr. 2.3. The motif appears to have been picked up by Latin authors as *munera Veneris*, as at Catullus 68a.10. Oliver (2015) uses the Callisto episode in Book 2 of the *Metamorphoses* to discuss how, in the rare instances that Latin texts discuss female homoeroticism, there is an attempt to reconcile female-female desire with a phallocentric model of intercourse, something that Oliver (2015, 297–298) diagnoses in the romance between Iphis and Ianthe.

63. Ingleheart 2015, 2, 3 note 2; see Halperin 2002, 16.

queer women (broadly defined) who love women, the sources for such companionship are thin on the ground: the life and poetry of the Greek poetess Sappho (including Ovid's portrayal of her in *Heroides* 15),[64] *Met.* 9, Juvenal's second and sixth *Satires*, and a smattering of Martial's epigrams.[65] These are among the only extant sources for ancient female homosexuality.[66] In this light, not surprisingly scholars and laypeople alike have sought to reclaim one of the most positive portrayals, Iphis and Ianthe, as progenitive lesbian icons.[67] It is socially and politically convenient and necessary to identify Iphis (and possibly also Ianthe) as something akin to modern lesbians as sources of legitimization and community.

I do not deny or belittle the importance of such modes of thought, but seek to expand upon them and to recognize that the issues of temporal isolation which women who love women once sought to resolve by connecting with their classical ancestors can extend just as much to modern trans people, and indeed to queer people more broadly defined. As much as lesbians have striven to discover their identity in the past, so too trans people face a similar quandary. Reclamations of Iphis and Caeneus as progenitors of modern trans identities are not especially revolutionary in popular and internet media,[68] such as academic blogs and online journals (e.g., Maisel 2019), but these reclamations, especially with a conscious awareness of their importance to not only academic but also social matters, have not yet entered traditional published scholarship.

To ignore a scholarly interpretation of Iphis and Ianthe as trans is to delegitimize the lens of trans-focused scholarship where it extends beyond the safe parameters of the modern world. I propose a polyvalent interpretation of such a myth: the past and ongoing scholarship, which sees Iphis and Caeneus as women

---

64. Although there is a debate surrounding the authorship of the *Epistula Sapphus*, Baca (1971), Kirfel (1969), and Showerman and Goold (1977) conclude that it is Ovidian, although Baca considers it separate from the rest of the *Heroides*.

65. Esp. Martial 1.90, 7.67, 7.70; see Butrica 2013, 247–262.

66. See Schachter in Ingleheart 2015, 39–55.

67. E.g., Hallett 1997, 207–220, and Brooten 1996, 3–4, 18–22.

68. E.g., literary fiction, such as Ali Smith's *Girl meets boy*, where protagonist Anthea Gunn's incipient relationship with the gender-ambiguous Robin Goodfellow is first presented to the reader via a plain narration of Ovid's tale of Iphis and Ianthe, followed by a chatty exegesis of the tale by the couple in bed (2018, 86–101). Both Iphis's and Ianthe's queerness is discussed, in consciously oblique terms, and Smith's couple later take on the identities of Iphis and Ianthe, whom they variously call "the messenger girls" and "the messenger boys" (2018, 133–137). For queer receptions of Ovid in *Girl meets boy*, see Mitchell 2013, Ziv 2014, Coppola 2015. Cf. also a host of amateur online fan fiction about Iphis (e.g., Halja 2014, Parizaad [orphan_account] 2016, odiko_ptino 2018) and Caeneus (e.g., deathbyvalentine 2017, ShanaStoryteller 2017), as well as tumblr comment chains about Caeneus (e.g. https://web.archive.org/web/20200818121618/https://jezebelgoldstone.tumblr.com/post/161905280778/ozandtherealboy-thrillingest).

who are masculinized due to the power of Roman patriarchy and recognizes Iphis's sexuality as essentially a 'deformulated lesbianism,' is not to be discredited, but neither are the present and future inquiries into their (and other characters') transness.

V Conclusion

The saliency of Iphis and Caeneus has proven to be a large obstacle to reading them as trans. Very few narratives from the ancient world feature the same sort of sustained gender transformations as Ovid's poem; even in the *Metamorphoses*, there are at best only seven transformations, as Lateiner (2009) suggests. Among these narratives,[69] Iphis and Caeneus clearly stand out as different and more developed, with their gender transformations being central to their stories. However, common in Latin literature is the use of gendered language as insult; in invective we see countless examples of effeminized men and fewer, but still numerous, examples of masculinized women. This is the sort of gender play that Filippo Carlà-Uhink (2017) has problematically called the "transgender discourse" and which is not quite like the affirmative way that Ovid tells the stories of Iphis and Caeneus. There are jokes and wordplays in Ovid's trans narratives, but Iphis's and Caeneus's genders are not the butt of these jokes; the framing of Ovid's tales is not invective against these men, but rather the story of how they came to be how they are.

We may examine as a point of comparison, for example, another literary character who is anatomically female and participates in the masculine world: Martial's Philaenis. A reclamation of Philaenis as some flavor of trans is not impossible,[70] as she performs a range of actions that Martial calls masculine—*pedicatio*, handball, wrestling, weightlifting (7.67), penetrative vaginal sex (7.70); but masculinity is not the same as being a man. Martial makes no effort to present Philaenis as a man, even claiming that she misunderstands masculinity (*di mentem tibi dent tuam, Philaeni, / cunnum lingere quae putas virile* ["May the gods give you some sense, Philaenis, you who thinks it a manly thing to lick cunt," 7.67.16–17]). As Boehringer has discussed, Philaenis is an object of disgust and anti-eroticism, not a man

---

69. Studies, such as Adkins 2014 and Blood 2019, have, for instance, examined the transness of the Roman priesthood of the *galli*.

70. To the best of my knowledge, there exists no literature that reclaims Philaenis as a trans man, either in traditionally published literature or fan fiction. Perhaps some *tribades* could fit within a capacious term like trans, but the hostility of the literature directed at them makes this a very difficult job. Philaenis is often described as a lesbian or masculine woman in scholarship; see Boehringer 2007, 333–335. Note that Boehringer is somewhat hostile to reclamation of ancient people using modern sexual and gender categories.

or even a butch lesbian.[71] Martial places Philaenis into the category of *tribades*, who are women who take an active, penetrative role in sex with both men and other women (Williams 2010, 233–235); however, this category does not fit Iphis and Caeneus. Ovid calls them both *viri* (e.g., 9.723, 12.204), not, like Philaenis, people who cannot understand maleness. There is no explicit sexual aspect to Caeneus's tale, although, as I have shown, Ovid colors his story with liberal sexual imagery, and although Iphis does eventually sexually penetrate a woman, he does as a man, not an oversexed woman.[72] Unlike Philaenis, Iphis and Caeneus clearly understand how to be a *vir* in the bedroom. The *tribas*, then, like her cousin the *cinaedus* whose sexual exploits lie beyond the bounds of this article, is a stock character of Roman opprobrium, a negatively masculinized woman,[73] not a trans man in the same way as Iphis and Caeneus.

This counter example can serve to illustrate what I do mean by trans man, as the differences between Philaenis, on the one hand, and Iphis and Caeneus, on the other, are more significant than any similarities that they share. As stated at the beginning of this article, I am not interested in making definitive comments about the lived gender experiences of Roman people. If there were trans people in the ancient world, I suggest that reconstructing their lives from our fragmentary and hostile evidence would be extremely difficult, if not impossible. I have strived to apply the broad category of trans to Iphis and Caeneus and to see whether it fits, and I believe it does. Unlike Philaenis, who is a 'real' *tribas* in 'real' Rome as far as Martial's poetic world presents, Iphis and Caeneus are fictional creations who live in the mythical world of Ovid's unreal *Metamorphoses*. By locating these men in the poetic landscape of the *Metamorphoses*, Ovid can write the rules and create a presentation of Iphis and Caeneus as two positively received trans men, without the need to situate them in contemporary Roman reality where stricter gender rules may have made positively evaluated transness harder to achieve. The fictive world of the *Metamorphoses* represents a unique site for the sort of gender play and metamorphosis that enable Iphis and Caeneus to be examined through a trans lens. Repeatedly, Ovid achieves corporeal transformations that were largely impossible to achieve through Roman science and medicine, most of which would be equally impossible in the modern day. What we would term gender reassignment or confirmation surgery is perhaps alluded to by Pliny (*HN* 7.36),[74] and so it does

---

71. See Boehringer 2014, esp. 381–384, and 2018.

72. Ormand (2005, 91–92) explicitly states that tribadism is not a good model for explaining Iphis and Ianthe's relationship.

73. For the links between the *tribas* and the *cinaedus*, see Williams 2010, 333–335.

74. See also Diodorus Siculus 32.10.2–9, who lists the surgery performed on what could be identified as two trans men: Diophantus and Callon. See Langlands 2002 on this passage.

not seem too fantastical to suggest that Ovid's presentation of Iphis and Caeneus originates in something 'real' in the Roman world; but, like the relationship between Ovid's self-professed *usus* ("experience") and the advice of the *Ars amatoria*,[75] the line between reality and poetry is hard to trace.

Ovid's *Metamorphoses* is a poem about change, but, as long recognized, these changes are often only external. Famously, Lycaon is *notus feritate* ("known for his wildness," 1.198) even as a human and has a name that evokes λύκος ("wolf"). It comes as no surprise, then, to the alert reader when he becomes a wild wolf (*Met.* 1.233–239):

> exululat frustraque loqui conatur; ab ipso
> colligit os rabiem, solitaeque cupidine caedis
> vertitur in pecudes et nunc quoque sanguine gaudet.   235
> in villos abeunt vestes, in crura lacerti;
> fit lupus et veteris servat vestigia formae:
> canities eadem est [...]
> [...] eadem feritatis imago est.

He howls and tries in vain to speak: his maw gathers fury from itself and, with his usual lust for death, he turns on the sheep and now he delights in blood. His clothes turn into shaggy fur, his arms turn into legs; he becomes a wolf and retains traces of his former body: his grey hair is the same, the echo of his wildness is the same.

In much the same way, Ovid's Iphis and Caeneus, in their transformations, assume externalities that more accurately represent their internal realities. Their paths to, and experiences of, manhood are different, but both Iphis and Caeneus unambiguously occupy a male gender by the end of their narratives. This is totally in keeping with the way that metamorphosis functions in the *Metamorphoses*. As Leonard Barkan (1986, 203) says, "The business of metamorphosis, then, is to make flesh of the metaphors." In both cases, Ovid has taken traditional mythology and adapted it in such a way as not only to remove doubt of Iphis's and Caeneus's genders, but also to reinforce their maleness. To follow Giaccherini's (2005, 62) proposal of the "integrity of the self that remains," both Iphis and Caeneus are integrally men; their

---

75. *Ars am.* 1.29: *usus opus movet hoc* ("Experience drives this work"), which is usually understood to mean that Ovid's love advice comes from a place of personal experience. As Hollis (1977, 37) suggests, we should take this claim with a pinch of salt in light of Ovid's later comments, e.g., *Tr.* 2.355–356: *magnaque pars mendax operum est et ficta meorum: / plus sibi permisit compositore suo* ("A large part of my work is a lie and is made up; it allowed more to itself that to its author").

exteriors subtly shift (although, for Ovid, these are very understated metamorphoses), but their ontological self remains fixed.[76]

Bibliographical References

Primary Literature

deathbyvalentine. 2017. "Caeneus." *Tumblr.* https://web.archive.org/web/20200818140808/https://deathbyvalentine.tumblr.com/post/156846462104/poseidon-you-loved-a-boy-like-me-a-boy-whos. (accessed 15 October 2021)
Halja. 2014. "A Girl on Fire for a Girl." *Archive of Our Own.* https://web.archive.org/web/20200818140941/https://archiveofourown.org/works/1179829. (accessed 12 October 2021)
odiko_ptino. 2018. "Visibility." *Archive of Our Own.* https://web.archive.org/web/20200818141032/https://archiveofourown.org/works/17029455. (accessed 21 October 2021)
Parizaad (orphan_account). 2016. "viola canina." *Archive of Our Own.* https://web.archive.org/web/20200818141116/https://archiveofourown.org/works/8648908?view_adult=true. (accessed 1 October 2021)
ShanaStoryteller. 2017. "Gods and Monsters, parts X, XIII and XVI." *Tumblr.* https://web.archive.org/web/20200818135155/https://shanastoryteller.tumblr.com/post/160679981930/your-athena-made-me-cry-id-like-you-to-know-and; and, https://web.archive.org/web/20200818135501/https://shanastoryteller.tumblr.com/post/162270604730/i-just-read-everything-in-your-gods-and-monsters; and, https://web.archive.org/web/20200818135604/https://shanastoryteller.tumblr.com/post/163159689655/your-caeneus-and-poseidon-fics-made-me-weep-will. (all accessed 19 October 2021)
Smith, Ali. 2018. *Girl meets boy.* Edinburgh: Canongate.

Secondary Literature

Adams, James N. 1990. *The Latin Sexual Vocabulary.* Second edition. Baltimore: Johns Hopkins University Press.
Adkins, Evelyn W. 2014. "*Rudis Locutor*: Speech and Self-Fashioning in Apuleius' *Metamorphoses*." Ph.d. diss., University of Michigan.
Ahl, Frederick. 1985. *Metaformations: Soundplay and Wordplay in Ovid and Other Classical Poets.* Ithaca: Cornell University Press.
American Psychiatric Association, 2013. *Diagnostic and Statistical Manual of Mental Disorders.* Fifth edition. Arlington: American Psychiatric Association.
Anderson, William S. 1996 [1972]. *Ovid's Metamorphoses: Books 1–5.* Norman, OK: University of Oklahoma Press.
Baca, Albert R. 1971. "Ovid's Epistle from Sappho to Phaon (*Heroides* 15)." *TAPA* 102: 29–38.

---

76. This article was first presented at the conference "'Becoming' and the Roman World" (2019) and was the inspiration for an interactive workshop entitled "In-Queering Minds: Finding Modern LGBTQ+ Identities in Ovid" (2020); my thanks go to the organizers of both events and to the participants for their feedback. Thanks also go to Jennifer Ingleheart and to Sophie Ngan for their support and feedback, as well as to the editor and the anonymous reader at *Helios*. Finally, I thank Chris Mowat for their support and for providing a trans perspective on this piece.

Barish, Sasha. 2018. "Iphis' Hair, Io's Reflection, and the Gender Dysphoria of the *Metamorphoses*." *Eidolon*. https://eidolon.pub/iphis-hair-io-s-reflection-and-the-gender-dysphoria-of-the-metamorphoses-4b75c1ba38d7. (accessed 15 October 2021)

Barkan, Leonard. 1986. *The Gods Made Flesh: Metamorphosis and the Pursuit of Paganism*. New Haven: Yale University Press.

Barthes, Roland. 1974. *S/Z: An Essay*. English translation by Roland Miller. New York: Hill and Wang. (Originally published as *S/Z* [Paris: Editions du Seuil, 1973])

Begum-Lees, Rebecca. 2020. "Que(e)r(y)ing Iphis' Transformation in Ovid's *Metamorphoses*." In Alison Surtees and Jennifer Dyer, eds., *Exploring Gender Diversity in the Ancient World*, 106–117. Edinburgh: Edinburgh University Press.

Blood, H. Christian. 2019. "*Sed illae puellae*: Transgender Studies and Apuleius's *The Golden Ass*." *Helios* 46: 163–188.

Boehringer, Sandra. 2007. *L'homosexualité féminine dans l'Antiquité grecque et romaine*. Paris: Les Belles Lettres.

Boehringer, Sandra. 2014. "What Is Named by the Name 'Philaenis'? Gender, Function and Authority of an Antonomastic Figure." In Mark Masterson, Nancy Rabinowitz, and Jaes E. Robson, eds., *Sex in Antiquity: Exploring Gender and Sexuality in the Ancient World*, 374–393. New York: Routledge.

Boehringer, Sandra. 2018. "Not a Freak but a Jack-in-the-Box: Philaenis in Martial, *Epigram* VII, 67." *Archimède* 5: 83–94.

Bömer, Franz. 1977. *P. Ovidius Naso: Metamorphosen: Buch VIII–IX*. Heidelberg: Universitätsverlag Winter.

Brooten, Bernadette J. 1996. *Love between Women: Early Christian Responses to Female Homoeroticism*. Chicago: The University of Chicago Press.

Butrica, James L. 2013. "Some Myths and Anomalies in the Study of Roman Sexuality." In Beert C. Verstraete and Vernon Provencal, eds., *Same-Sex Desire and Love in Greco-Roman Antiquity and in the Classical Tradition of the West*, 209–270. New York: Routledge.

Carlà-Uhink, Filippo. 2017. "'Between the Human and the Divine': Cross-Dressing and Transgender Dynamics in the Graeco-Roman World." In Domitilla Campanile, Filippo Carlà-Uhink, and Margherita Facella, eds., *TransAntiquity: Cross-Dressing and Transgender Dynamics in the Ancient World*, 3–37. Abingdon-Oxon-New York: Routledge.

Clarke, Hannah. 2019. "Queer Classics: Survey of LGBTQ+ Classicists Reveals Community and Continuity." *Eidolon*. https://eidolon.pub/queer-classics-b84819356f74. (accessed 11 October 2021)

Coppola, Maria M. 2015. "'A Whole Spectrum of Colours New to the Eye': Gender Metamorphoses and Identity Frescoes in Girl meets boy and How to Be Both by Ali Smith'. *Textus* 4: 169–185.

Corbeill, Anthony. 2015. *Sexing the World: Grammatical Gender and Biological Sex in Ancient Rome*. Princeton: Princeton University Press.

Dolansky, Fanny L. 1997. "Coming of Age in Rome: The History and Social Significance of Assuming the *Toga Virilis*." Ph.d. diss., University of Victoria.

Ernout, Alfred. 1957. *Philologica II*. Paris: Klincksieck.

Forbes Irving, Paul M. C. 1990. *Metamorphosis in Greek Myths*. Oxford: Clarendon Press.

Franklin, Lisa. 2018. "Life as an Iphis: Ancient and Modern Perspectives on Your Hopeless Gay Crush." *Eidolon*. https://eidolon.pub/life-as-an-iphis-fbdecf92fbe1. (accessed 12 October 2021)

Freas, Debra. 2018. "Da *femina ne sim*: Gender, Genre and Violence in Ovid's Caenis Episode." *CJ* 114: 60–84.
Giaccherini, Enrico. 2005. "Metamorphosis, Science Fiction and the Dissolution of the Self." In Carla Dente et al., eds., *Proteus: The Language of Metamorphosis*, 62–70. Burlington, VT: Ashgate Publishing. 62–70.
Gleason, Maud W. 1995. *Making Men: Sophists and Self-Presentation in Ancient Rome*. Princeton: Princeton University Press.
Hallett, Judith P. 1997. "Female Homoeroticism and the Denial of Roman Reality in Latin Literature." In Hallett and Skinner 1997, 255–273.
Hallett, Judith P., and Marilyn B. Skinner, eds. 1997. *Roman Sexualities*. Princeton: Princeton University Press.
Halperin, David M., 2002. *How to Do the History of Homosexuality*. Chicago: The University of Chicago Press.
Harrill, J. Albert. 2002. "Coming of Age and Putting on Christ: The *Toga Virilis* Ceremony, Its Paraenesis, and Paul's Interpretation of Baptism in Galatians." *NT* 44: 252–277.
Hill, Donald E. 1999. *Ovid: Metamorphoses, IX–XII*. Warminster: Aris & Phillips.
Hollis, Adrian S. 1977. *Ovid: Ars amatoria, Book 1*. Oxford: Oxford University Press.
Hirschfeld, Magnus. 1923. "Die intersexuelle Konstitution." *Jahrbuch für sexuellen Zwischenstufen* 23 : 3–27.
Ingleheart, Jennifer, ed. 2015. *Ancient Rome and the Construction of Modern Homosexual Identities*. Oxford: Oxford University Press.
Kamen, Deborah. 2012. "Naturalized Desires and the Metamorphosis of Iphis." *Helios* 39: 21–36.
Kirfel, Ernest-Alfred. 1969. *Untersuchungen zur Briefform der Heroides Ovids*. Bern: Haupt.
Langlands, Rebecca. 2002. "'Can You Tell What It is Yet?' Descriptions of Sex Change in Ancient Literature." *Ramus* 31: 91–110.
Lateiner, Donald. 2009. 'Transsexuals and Transvestites in Ovid's *Metamorphoses*." In Thorsten Fögen and Mireille M. Lee, eds., *Bodies and Boundaries in Graeco-Roman Antiquity*, 125–154. Berlin and New York: Walter de Gruyter.
Lawrence, Elizabeth A. 1994. "The Centaur: Its History and Meaning in Human Culture." *The Journal of Popular Culture* 27: 57–68.
Maisel, L. K. M. 2019. "Women Are Made, But from What? Modern and Ancient Trans Antagonism." *Eidolon*. https://eidolon.pub/women-are-made-but-from-what-modern-and-ancient-trans-antagonism-17512e3987ff . (accessed 11 October 2021)
Mitchell, Kaye. 2013. "Queer Metamorphoses: *Girl meets boy* and the Futures of Queer Fiction." In Monica Germana and Emily Horton, eds., *Ali Smith: Contemporary Critical Perspectives*, 61–74. London: A&C Black.
Mynors, Roger A. B. 1958. *C. Valerii Catulli Carmina*. Oxford: Clarendon Press.
Nagle, Betty Rose. 1984. "'Amor, Ira,' and Sexual Identity in Ovid's 'Metamorphoses.'" *ClAnt* 3: 236–255.
Oliven, John F. 1965. *Sexual Hygeine and Pathology: A Manual for the Physician and the Professions*. Philadelphia: Lippincott.
Oliver, Jen H. 2015. "*Oscula iungit nec moderata satis nec sic a virgine danda*: Ovid's Callisto Episode, Female Homoeroticism, and the Study of Ancient Sexuality." *AJP* 136: 281–312.
Ormand, Keith. 2005. "Impossible Lesbians in Ovid's *Metamorphoses*." In Ronnie Ancona and Ellen Greene, eds., *Gendered Dynamics in Latin Love Poetry*, 79–112. Baltimore: Johns Hopkins University Press.

Papanikolaou, Dimitris. 2014. *"Σαν κ' εμένα καμωμένοι": Ο ομοφυλόφιλος Καβάφης και η ποιητική της σεξουαλικότητας*. Αθήνα: Πατάκης.
Pintabone, Diane T. 2002. "Ovid's Iphis and Ianthe: When Girls Won't Be Girls." In Nancy S. Rabinowitz and Lisa Auanger, eds., *Among Women: From the Homosocial to the Homoerotic in the Ancient World*, 256–285. Austin: University of Texas Press.
Preston, Keith. 1916. "Studies in the Diction of the *Sermo Amatorius* in Roman Comedy." Ph.d. diss., University of Chicago.
Raval, Shilpa. 2002. "Cross-Dressing and 'Gender Trouble' in the Ovidian Corpus." *Helios* 29: 149–172.
Rawson, Beryl. 1999. *The Roman Family in Italy*. Oxford: Oxford University Press.
Saller, Richard P. 1987. "Men's Age at Marriage and Its Consequences in the Roman Family." *CP* 82: 21–34.
Showerman, Grant, and G. P. Goold. 1977. *Ovid: Heroides, Amores*. Second edition. Cambridge, MA: Harvard University Press.
Spies, Alfons. 1930. "*Militat omnis amans;* Ein Beitrag zur Bildersprache der antiken Erotik." Ph.d. diss., Universität Tübingen.
Treggiari, Susan. 1991. *Roman Marriage: Iusti Coniuges from the Time of Cicero to the Time of Ulpian*. Oxford: Oxford University Press.
Walker, Jonathan. 2006. "Before the Name: Ovid's Deformulated Lesbianism." *CompLit* 58: 205–222.
Walters, Jonathan. 1993. "'No More Than a Boy': The Shifting Construction of Masculinity from Ancient Greece to the Middle Ages." *Gender & History* 5: 20–33.
Walters, Jonathan. 1997. "Invading the Roman Body: Manliness and Impenetrability in Roman Thought." In Hallett and Skinner 1997, 29–47.
Wheeler, Stephen M. 1997. "Changing Names: The Miracle of Iphis in Ovid 'Metamorphoses' 9." *Phoenix* 51: 190–202.
Williams, Craig A. 2010. *Roman Homosexuality*. Second edition. Oxford: Oxford University Press.
Ziogas, Ioannis. 2013. *Ovid and Hesiod: The Metamorphosis of the Catalogue of Women*. Cambridge: Cambridge University Press.
Ziv, Amalia. 2014. "*Girl meets boy*: Cross-Gender Queer Sex and the Promise of Pornography." *Sexualities* 17: 885–905.

Notes on Contributors

MARIA COMBATTI completed her Ph.D. in Classics at Columbia University in 2020. Her research interests range from Presocratic philosophy, Hippocratic medicine, and Greek tragedy to Hellenistic poetry, especially Callimachus. Her current book project focuses on intersections between gender and environment in Greek tragedy.

ALEXANDRA LEEWON SCHULTZ is a research fellow in Classics at the University of Cambridge. Her research examines the politics of literature and the history of knowledge in Greco-Roman antiquity, with special interests in ancient libraries, gender and sexuality, and feminist theory. Her current book project reimagines the history of libraries in the Hellenistic world, thereby changing how we understand the relationship between knowledge and power in Greco-Roman antiquity.

J. L. WATSON is a doctoral student in Latin Literature at Durham University. His thesis is on the psycho-linguistic presentation of extreme sexual taboo (incest and bestiality) in Ovid's *Metamorphoses*. His research interests focus on queer and non-queer sex, gender, and sexuality in the ancient world and its modern receptions. He has previously published on the queer reception of ancient Greek sculpture in the poetry of C. P. Cavafy and is preparing an edition and translation of Cavafy's *Poetic and Ethical Notes*.

www.ingramcontent.com/pod-product-compliance
Lightning Source LLC
Chambersburg PA
CBHW020948090426
42736CB00010B/1314